CLIFFORD PEARSON · PHOTOGRAPHY BY BRYAN WHITNEY

INDONESIA
Design and Culture

JAVA · SUMATRA · SULAWESI · BALI

THE MONACELLI PRESS

TABLE OF CONTENTS

First published in the United States of America in 1998 by
The Monacelli Press, Inc.
10 East 92nd Street, New York, New York 10128.

Library of Congress Cataloging-in-Publication Data
Pearson, Clifford A.
Indonesia : design and culture, Java, Sumatra, Sulawesi, Bali /
Clifford Pearson ; photography by Bryan Whitney.
p.   cm.
ISBN 1-58093-012-3
1. Interior decoration—Indonesia. 2. Exoticism in architecture—
Indonesia. 3. Design—Indonesia. 4. Indonesia—Social life and
customs. I. Whitney, Bryan. II. Title.
NK2080.A1P43   1998
745'.09598—dc21   98-19131

Printed and bound in Hong Kong

Designed by Fahrenheit

ACKNOWLEDGMENTS

A book such as this one requires the help of a large number of backstage actors, many of whom played very important roles. I would like to thank all of them and identify a few.

Without the support of publisher Gianfranco Monacelli and the guidance (and enthusiasm) of editor Andrea Monfried, there would be no book. They were there when *Indonesia: Design and Culture* was but a hope and a whim. Thanks also to Paul Montie of Fahrenheit, whose book design created such a spectacular showcase for Bryan Whitney's photographs and my words.

Successful journeys usually require the help of expert guides and this book was blessed with a few great ones. At the top of the list is Andyan Rahardja, who seems to know everyone of any importance in Indonesia and was generous enough with his time, knowledge, and connections to open many doors for us during the entire gestation period of this project. His wife, Diane, and brother Ardyan also graciously pitched in whenever needed.

In Jakarta, Monica Ginting Soedibyo was our master coordinator, etiquette instructor, and mother hen who made sure we got where we needed to, spoke to all the right people, and ate a good bowl of *soto ayam* in the evening. Helping her cope with us were her husband, Bambang, and computer-savvy son, Dadi, who relayed E-mail between Jakarta and New York. Hendro Prabowo and Prasetyo Budi took us around Yogyakarta, central Java, and Sumatra, making sure we saw where the poor, as well as the affluent, live.

Many thanks to Suntana of the Indonesian Institute of Architects and Mohammad Danisworo, who provided advice on modern architecture in Indonesia.

Alex Hardjo was another indispensable friend, who opened not only his own Red Door and Green Door to us, but those of many fascinating people in Jakarta.

Equally important was Restu Iman Sari, who helped us navigate Jakarta's art world and provided contacts in her native Sumatra. Thanks also to Dedi Sjahrir Panigoro, who provided an elegant roof over our heads in Bukittinggi, and Christophe Keramaris and Yusuf Ijsseldijk at the Bukittinggi Novotel, who shared their knowledge and love of the Minangkabau people.

In Bali, Andrea Phillips and her husband, Nyoman, were our guiding spirits for our first trip and have remained helpful ever since. Leonard Lueras was another wonderful host who arranged everything from frog dances to introductions. Iskandar Wawo-Runtu and his father, Wija, also gave generously of their time and understanding of Bali.

We would also like to thank Mira Alwi Szarata of GHM Resorts in Bali for arranging accommodations and to Garuda International for helping with airfare.

In the United States, Wayne Forrest of the American-Indonesian Chamber of Commerce provided expert advice throughout this project and was sharp enough to catch a few errors in our manuscript before they got into print. Also helping out with contacts were Bridget Brown, Luisa Kreisberg, Wendy Moonan, Terry Schaefer, and Suzanne Stephens.

We also want to thank Ardiyanto, Christopher Carlisle, Popo Danes, David Handley, Jaya Ibrahim, Ratina Moegiono, Nyoman Nuarta and his family, Professor A. D. Pirous, Sang Made Puanya (a.k.a. Skeleton Man), Made Punia, John Saunders, Nigel Simmonds, Simon of Ubud, Tara Sosrowardoyo, Goenawan Widjaya, and Amri Yahya.

Of course, thanks also go to everyone who welcomed us into their homes to take photographs and share these special places with our readers.

Finally, I must recognize my debt to my wife, Lily Chin, who put up with all the craziness that came with this project.

INDONESIA: CULTURE

I fell in love with Indonesia from a distance. The place was Amsterdam and I was just eleven years old, on vacation in Europe with my family. Our guidebook had recommended a restaurant called Bali for a "traditional" Indonesian *rijsttafel*, so we made a reservation. It was love at first bite. The colorful array of a dozen little dishes presented on a long wooden board captured my imagination—turmeric-coated chicken with spicy peanut sauce, anise-scented beef in an onion and tomato stew, fish in curry, curls of coconut meat, crispy threads of onions, peanuts, and a variety of items about which I could only wonder. On the walls were black-and-white photographs of Balinese princes and princesses, terraced hillsides sprouting wisps of young rice, elaborately carved temple gates, bug-eyed demons incarnated as wooden masks, and offerings of rice balls held in woven banana-leaf baskets. Add to that the waiters and waitresses dressed in richly colored sarongs and I was enthralled.

Only years later was I to learn that Bali the restaurant was but an image of Bali the island, filtered through the eyes and imaginations of Western colonialists. Our "traditional" *rijsttafel* was an invention of Dutch traders whose appetites demanded much more than the simple meals of rice, a little meat, and a few condiments that most Indonesians ate. The restaurant had many of the details correct—the sarongs and the *wayang kulit* shadow puppets, for example, were authentic Indonesian—but the spirit was hyphenated: Dutch-Indonesian. This was Bali for tourists, Indonesia served up for westerners in thrall with the exotic East.

The difference between the "real" and the "imagined" Indonesia is of great concern to some visitors to the country. These well-traveled foreigners desperately search out the "real" Java, the "real" Barong dances, the "real" Bugis pirates, and especially the "real" Bali. But in Indonesia, the distinction between real and imagined, substance and spirit, commonplace and magical is usually left vague. Opposites are merely flip sides of the same coin; you can't have one without the other. I have overheard "serious" travelers bemoan the oh-so-common practice of Indonesians selling T-shirts emblazoned with images of shadow puppets or hawking cheap imitations of ancient wood carvings. Indonesians are much less troubled by all this. They are comfortable with the duality of everything. True and false sit side by side in Indonesian culture without one denying the other.

In Bali there are two worlds—*sekala* and *niskala* (the material and the immaterial)—that are present in everything. There is what is visible in light and what is

only seen in shadow. The famous *wayang kulit* shadow-puppet plays are manifestations of this duality. A *dalang* (puppeteer) sits cross-legged behind a screen with an oil lantern and manipulates cowhide puppets to tell a story—usually a traditional Hindu tale from the *Ramayana* or *Mahabharata*. Most of the audience sits on the other side of the screen and

east to west and encompasses the aboriginal Dayaks of Borneo, who once hunted heads, and jet-setters in Jakarta, who sip cappuccino. How can you fit all that in one book?

But this book isn't intended to be the definitive volume on Indonesian architecture or design. It is rather an overview, a colorful skimming of a few places and ideas. The houses and buildings shown here offer just a glimpse of the true richness of Indonesian design. What I have assembled is an introduction to a country that, despite its size and rich culture, remains little known to the rest of the world. To most Americans, Java is a computer language, Sumatra is a type of coffee, Komodo is a dragon, and Bali is a place out of a Broadway show tune.

For a country its size, Indonesia had a remarkably low profile until its recent economic and political troubles made front-page news. The *New York Times,* which has one of the most extensive networks of foreign bureaus of any United States newspaper, has no reporters based in Indonesia. Thumbing through a magazine recently, I came across another reminder of how Indonesia doesn't even register on most Americans' cultural radar screens. It was an ad for a company selling audio tapes and books that teach foreign languages. "Learn Another Language on Your Own!" promised the ad. Forty different languages were listed,

watches not the actual puppets but the shadows thrown by the puppets. In this way, the shadow world becomes visible.

If you want, however, you can watch the show from behind the *dalang* and see how it's all done. Go back and forth from one side of the screen to the other—it's up to you. Backstage and out front are just alternate vantage points for viewing the same story. One is no better or more "real" than the other.

Indonesia is full of such dualities: old and new, traditional and modern, commercial and sacred, playful and serious, repressive and free. Contrasts abound. Glass-and-steel skyscrapers are erected behind bamboo scaffolding. A Kentucky Fried Chicken joint sits next door to a roadside *warung* selling *soto ayam* (chicken soup). Whitney Houston songs are played after *gamelan* music.

Discussing Indonesian culture or Indonesian anything is a gross simplification. The country comprises 13,000 to 17,000 islands (depending on which source you cite and whether it is low or high tide), several hundred different languages (some of which have three or more ways of being spoken, depending on the caste of the people doing the speaking), myriad religions, and countless regions.

So the very notion of an Indonesian style is, of course, pure fiction. Whenever I mentioned the topic of my book to people familiar with Indonesia, they invariably smiled at my gall, naïveté, and ignorance. Indonesia is the fourth largest country in the world with nearly 210 million people. It is the largest Muslim nation in the world. It stretches more than three thousand miles

including Bulgarian, Catalan, Estonian, Haitian Creole, Lakota, Latvian, Lithuanian, Serbo-Croatian, Tagalog, Thai, and Vietnamese. But no Bahasa Indonesian!

Straddling some of the busiest trade routes in the world, Indonesia has welcomed strangers for centuries. More than fifteen hundred years ago, ships crossing the Indian Ocean brought Hinduism and then Buddhism along with traders and fortune seekers. In the fifteenth century, Arab seamen exported Islam and frankincense. One hundred years later came the European powers—first the Portuguese, then the Dutch and the British—in search of spices worth their weight in gold.

In the days before refrigerators and freeze-drying, preserving food was a major concern. Back then, salting, pickling, and drying were the major ways of keeping food edible between deliveries, during long winters, and on great journeys. But if you've ever eaten beef jerky or salt pork for a couple of days in a row, you know how desperate people can get for some food

with real taste. Spices help retard spoilage, cover up the bad taste of partially spoiled food (which people through most of history have had to eat), and add flavor to everything. So it is no wonder that the people with money back then were willing to spend lots of it on spices. As it turns out, the spices Europeans loved the most—like clove, cinnamon, and nutmeg—grew only in a few parts of the Far East, which, of course, only made their prices that much more exorbitant. Control the islands where these precious spices came from and you would be very rich.

During much of the seventeenth century, the Dutch and British were at each other's throats, fighting for control of various parts of Asia and the New World. The Dutch had the upper hand for most of this period in Indonesia, but the English eventually took the lead in the Americas. Confirming these shifts in power, and highlighting the value of spices and Indonesia during

this period of empire building, was a little-known deal signed by Britain and Holland near the end of the century, which included a swap of islands. The Dutch received Run, one of the Moluccas Islands at the eastern end of the archipelago, prized as the only source of nutmeg in the world. In return, the British were granted control of a small island in the New World, which overlooked an excellent deep-water harbor but had few natural resources to extract and sell. The island was called Manhattan.

The peoples of Nusantara ("the land between the waters," which is what Indonesians call their country) adopted what they liked from the foreigners who came to trade and colonize—changing and shaping these things in the process. The resulting diversity in traditions, religions, and practices offers a superficial similarity to that of the United States. But while the cultural mosaic of America was pieced together by people who came from afar and settled down, that of Indonesia was developed from ideas brought from afar and adapted by the indigenous people. The result is both similar and different, familiar and surprising.

Indonesians are great believers in a panoply of spirits—demons, ghosts, witches, gods, and ancestors—who take up residence in inanimate objects. Rocks, trees, rivers, and mountains have spirits inside them, so it is wise to respect them and not abuse them. Buildings, too, are seen as living things, imbued with the spark of creation. When a house in Bali, for example, is completed, tradition calls for a special ceremony to be held before people can move in. Holy water is sprinkled about, offerings are made to the spirits, and a priest blows on the structure's main columns to breathe life into the house. It's a wonderful belief—that a house is more than the sum of its physical parts, that it has its own personality shaped but not totally determined by its creators. Like other living things, a house can grow and change over time. While it requires care and attention, it also gives back love and protection. Even in the prove-it-to-me, rational West, we know there is much truth to this view of the physical world. The best buildings always impress us with their spirit, their unique (and evolving) character.

Václav Havel, the president of the Czech Republic, once said in a speech that humankind today is living "a quiet life on the peak of a volcano" and called for everyone to find a humbler way of living. Indonesians have long lived on the peak of a volcano, both literally and figuratively. Nearly all of the country's islands are volcanic, making up a large part of the great chain of active volcanoes that geologists call the Ring of Fire. Starting with the infamous Krakatoa in the Sunda Strait between the Indonesian islands of Java and Sumatra, the Ring of Fire arcs for thousands of miles through the Pacific. (Krakatoa is the volcano that blew its top—and eleven cubic miles of ash and rock—into the stratosphere in 1883, affecting global weather for years and inspiring a Hollywood disaster movie a century later with the geographically incorrect title of *Krakatoa, East of Java*.)

Living as they do on the peak—or at least the slopes—of volcanoes, Indonesians have a deeper understanding of these restless mountains than Hollywood does. Rather than seeing them only as sources of destruction and evil, the people of Nusantara know that volcanoes also provide the fertile soil that nurtures life and, therefore, are owed respect and love. Indeed, in places like Bali the good forces in life come from Gunung Agung, the great volcanic mountain at the heart of the island, while evil spirits come from the ocean.

In a less literal way, Indonesia is living quietly on a political and social volcano. Because it is a nation of diverse peoples and religions, who have not always lived in peace with one another, it has often looked to strong rulers to hold it together. At certain times, when strong rule has failed or when latent social ills have surfaced, violent eruptions have engulfed the country. Such a time was 1965, the so-called Year of Living Dangerously (recorded by Hollywood in a movie of the same name), when the rule of President Sukarno began to crumble, and hundreds of thousands of Communists and innocent ethnic Chinese Indonesians were massacred in a wave of mob violence. For the past two decades, Indonesia has enjoyed an impressive surge in its gross domestic product, a burgeoning middle class, and political stability. But as seen in the protests and riots that toppled President Suharto in May 1998, as well as going conflicts in places such as East Timor (where an independence movement has been pitted against the Indonesian government since the 1970s) and Irian Jaya (where aboriginal people have protested destructive mining operations), and with some citizens calling for more democracy and labor rights, there is always the chance of something exploding.

I have tried to capture some of Indonesia's richness in this book. But pictures and words can only hint at the magical brew that is Indonesia. They can offer design inspirations that you may learn from and then transform, just as Indonesians have done with foreign ideas for centuries. And perhaps they can spark your imagination and lead you to explore further, just as an exotic meal did with an American kid in Amsterdam several decades ago.

Tschu Tschan Schika
Tsingtau Schika Schikok Bonin-I.
Gelbes M. Tschifu kiu Schikok (Jap.)
Pukou M. Tschisu Nagasaki kg Kagoschima
Nanking Tsang kg Kiuschiu M.
Su-tschou Schang-hai

Wuhu Hang-tschou
tsch Kiu-kiang Won-tschou-Str. Vulkan-I. Marianen Saipan
Fu-tschou Won-tschou Str. (Jap.) Guam zu Ver St.
Tschang-tschou Amoy Formosa v.N.A.
Kanton Swatoro Tai-nan J A P A N I S C H E

Hong-kong (Br.) Ehemaliger Deu
Macao (Port.)
Kwang-tschou-B. Olea Lamtrik
(Fr.) Jap Karolin
Kiung-tschou Philippinen
Hai-nan Lingayen I. Luzon (Japan.Mand
king Manila Palau-In. kolonialb
I. Mindoro Samar
Palawan Panay I.Ver.St.v.N.A.
Negros Mindanao
Zamboanga
Sandakan Djilolo St.David-I.
I. Labuan Brit. Sulu-I. (Halmahera)
Brunei Nord Sangi-I. Charles L. N.-Guin
Natuna-I. Borneo Celebes-S. Menado Ternate Geelvink-B. Geb. NEU-
Gorontalo Molukken GUINEA
Pontianak Makassar-Str. Sula- Seram Aru-In. Frederik H-I.
Buru Amboina
Bandjermasin Celebes Banda-S. Timorlaut
Sunda-S. Makassar Arafura-S.
atavia Delhi (Port.) Kap York
Surabaya Flores Palmerston ria-Golf Carpenta-Kap
Madura-I. Timor
Djokjakarta Sumbawa Kupang
Bali Lombok Sumba Cambridge AUSTRALIE
D. IND

INDONESIA: DESIGN

The notion of reducing all of Indonesian design to seven underlying principles is as immodest as the idea of writing a book on such a large place as Indonesia. On one level, of course, this is impossible; the diversity of cultures, languages, ethnic groups, social practices, customs, and traditions is too great to be neatly wrapped in a one-size-fits-all fabric. But I believe that identifying some of the common themes running through the arts, crafts, and architecture of the archipelago serves an important purpose. It provides a framework for us to look at the dizzying array of design found throughout Indonesia. While no framework is perfect or all-inclusive, a good one brings order to what at first might seem chaotic. Browsing through the houses and places in this book, the reader might find it useful to keep the following themes in mind.

1 INSIDE OUT The tropical climate of Indonesia has shaped an architecture in which outdoor spaces are often more important than indoor ones. In a country where it is hot and humid most of the time, relaxing and eating and even sleeping are usually more comfortable outdoors. And since flowers and plants grow in abundance everywhere, gardens are the cheapest and easiest way to decorate a home.

The key is creating outdoor rooms that are protected from the direct pounding of sun and rain. How this is done varies greatly from one place to another. Verandas, porches, overhanging roofs, and covered pavilions are just a few of the devices that are used. In Bali, the typical home is a compound of thatch-roofed pavilions open to breezes and views. A wall around the entire compound provides privacy and protection from

intruders, so few walls are needed inside the complex. In Borneo, long houses accommodating many families have front galleries stretching as much as three or four hundred feet. The covered gallery serves as the main corridor linking all of the individual apartments, but is also where domestic chores are done, where men relax with their carving, and where village meetings and performances take place.

Indoor rooms are often dark cool places, retreats from the sun. Small windows with wooden shutters or louvers are the norm. Rich fabrics, carved screens, and all sorts of crafts and artwork add color and visual interest to interiors.

2 **NATURAL MATERIALS** While metal roofs, concrete frames, and neon signs are becoming increasingly common, the best Indonesian architecture usually relies on natural materials—especially bamboo, various kinds of wood, *alang-alang* grass for thatching, and palm leaves. Most houses are post-and-beam timber construction, raised above the ground on wooden piles. In Bali and many parts of Java, houses sit on the ground on masonry foundations, and walls are often brick.

In the past, natural materials made sense because they were readily available and cheap. Today, metal roofs, Italian stone, and reflective glass are no longer as difficult to get as they once were, so the temptation to experiment with these "exotic" materials is great.

But bamboo, palm, coconut wood, grasses, hemp, clay, and locally made brick are the underpinnings of the different architectures of Indonesia. The way these materials are assembled and treated varies from place to place, but bringing out their nature is a shared goal of builders throughout the archipelago. Even in modern buildings, the best designs use natural materials where people can touch and appreciate them.

While materials such as tropical hardwoods are becoming too scarce and expensive to be commonly used, many others are still abundant. Bamboo, for example, grows remarkably fast, is cheap, and can be used in a multitude of ways (as logs, split as roof tiles, and split and woven as partitions). Natural materials are simply the aesthetic glue that holds much of Indonesia's eclectic architecture together.

3 **ORIENTATION** One of the terrible legacies of modern construction is its disregard for the basic principles of placing and orienting buildings on a site. Instead of carefully considering where the sun will rise and set, which directions the prevailing breezes blow from, and how natural features affect the character of a place, today's builders all too often rely on mechanical means to provide a comfortable indoor environment. Seal the building from the outdoors, then blast the interiors with air conditioning. Squeeze houses together in a suburban development, then make sure there are enough light fixtures to brighten the rooms where the sun doesn't shine. That's the attitude.

Traditional Indonesian design takes a very different approach. Keeping a building cool without air conditioning starts with properly orienting it to the sun and the winds. But in Indonesia (and, indeed, in many parts of Asia) orientation goes beyond purely practical concerns to encompass spiritual ones. In Bali, for example, houses and entire villages are laid out so their most sacred and important elements face the island's mountains, the source of life and power. Every part of a family compound has its proper position in relation to the Balinese-Hindu view of the universe. Building a house involves understanding a complex body of religious beliefs. Similarly, mosques are oriented toward Mecca. And almost every hotel room in Indonesia has an arrow (sometimes painted on the ceiling, sometimes placed in a dresser drawer) pointing the way to the holy city of Islam, so the devout know which way to direct their prayers.

Although the Chinese system of feng shui is not widely practiced in Indonesia, builders usually consider the impact of natural and supernatural forces on their structures. Superstition certainly plays a part in this process, as it does in design around the world (note the Western tradition of skipping the unlucky thirteen in numbering floors of modern skyscrapers). But Asian traditions often go beyond superstition and result in buildings that are well lit, properly shaded, and naturally ventilated. Appeasing the gods and spirits of a place somehow seems to help make a house or a temple more comfortable and attractive.

4 BOLD COMBINATIONS When it comes to color, form, and texture, Indonesians are fearless. Note the buffalo-horn shaped roofs resting on brilliantly painted carved-wood walls of houses in the Minangkabau region of Sumatra. Or the complex layering of batik sarong, colored sash, makeup, and elaborate jewelry of *legong* dancers. Whether you visit a typical Malay-style house in Java or a Toraja house in Sulawesi, you'll find colors and materials combined in ways that shouldn't work—but do.

5 BORROWING FROM OTHERS Having attracted traders, soldiers, missionaries, colonialists, and tourists for thousands of years, Indonesians have been exposed to all kinds of foreign influences. Taking ideas that started elsewhere and then adapting them as their own, Indonesians have become some of the best borrowers in the world. The trick lies in taking what's new and fusing it with their own sensibilities. The great monument of Borobudur, for example, takes its religious imagery from Indian Buddhism, but still has the indelible stamp of central Java all over it. Modern batik designs share the same character: European colors have been married to Javanese patterns.

6 EMBELLISHMENT Indonesian art has been called baroque in its treatment of surfaces and decoration. More is better than less. Elaboration is preferred over reserve. The old wood houses of Kudus in Java, for example, are covered in veritable jungles of intricate carvings. In Bali, Pengosekan-style paintings are dense with images of flora and fauna.

The three main religions in Indonesia—Islam, Hinduism, and Buddhism—all have artistic traditions that favor embellishment. The geometric complexity of much Islamic architecture, the kinetic multi-armed gods of Hindu sculpture, and the richly detailed surfaces of Buddhist paintings share a common urge toward filling all available space. This sensibility is perhaps reinforced by the riot of colors, forms, textures, and species of Indonesia's natural world. It's a jungle out there, and it seems to inspire Indonesian artists to be similarly lush in their work.

7 **TRADITION** No matter how much things have changed, Indonesian design is still rooted in strong traditions passed from one generation to another. Women in the Minang highlands of Sumatra still weave *songket* cloth spiked with gold thread using the same discontinuous supplementary-weft technique that their ancestors did hundreds of years ago. Although worn today only on special occasions, like weddings, *songket* remains a tangible link to the Minang people's past. In Irian Jaya, the Asmat carve remarkable ancestral poles that keep the past alive in the age-old methods used and in the stories depicted.

In villages and towns around the country most people still help build their own homes. Even those who live in big cities often return to their ancestral villages to pitch in when the family's house of origin needs repairing or rebuilding. Researching this book, I was struck by how involved most Indonesians are with the creation of their homes. Hiring an architect doesn't mean taking a backseat in the design process. A university professor in Bandung, for example, not only worked closely with his architect but went so far as to use the measurements from his own body as the basis for those of his house—an old Asian tradition.

In Indonesia traditions live on because many people still practice them, not because architects or cultural historians study them. Being alive, these traditions are still changing and evolving. New patterns or colors or materials might be used. Painters who once focused solely on religious themes might now turn their attention to secular subjects as well. But the artistic vocabulary used is most often one that their forefathers would understand.

This book presents an idiosyncratic view of a diverse country, seen through the eyes of a foreign author and a foreign photographer. While most style books and design publications focus almost exclusively on the built environment, I have tried to bring people back into the picture. You can't understand a house unless you know something about the people who live there. This is especially true in a place like Indonesia where everyone seems to be some kind of an artist, even if he or she earns an income from banking or making business deals. The roles of architect and client are often blurred here, with the owner of a house taking the lead in making design decisions.

And you can't understand Indonesia unless you know something about the people who make it their home: from a young man who carves bone for a living to a wealthy hotel operator, from the residents of a squatter community in Yogyakarta to a therapist whose advice column runs in the nation's largest newspaper, from Western expatriates to Javanese royalty. Whenever I hear talk of style, I always want to know "whose style," not "what style." Tell me about the builders as well as the buildings. Give me the stories of the people, not just descriptions of the places where they live, work, pray, trade, and play.

Java

JAKARTA

JAVA SEA

BANDUNG

MADURA ISLAND

BOROBUDUR   SOLO

YOGYAKARTA

SURABAYA

PRAMBANAN

INDIAN OCEAN

0   100 m

At first, the Whitney Houston incident seemed like one of those amusing anomalies that just happen but don't really mean much. We were in Bandung, a university town in west Java, photographing houses and doing research for this book. We had spent much of the day with an artist at his studio, being treated more as family than as strangers from abroad. Late in the afternoon, the artist's wife asked if we had any plans for the evening. No, we didn't. "Good. Why don't you join us tonight? We're having a tenth wedding anniversary party and would love to have you come." We were honored. The celebration took place at a fancy hotel and was anything but traditionally Javanese: the food was French, the guests international, and the attire downtown New York. When the band started playing, it too seemed like a typical hotel-lounge act doing covers of commercial hits from America. The lead singer was a young Indonesian woman, not much more than five feet tall and one hundred pounds. When she began to sing, though, a great big voice filled the room. It was Whitney Houston's. The pitch, the timbre, the remarkable clarity, the phrasing were—beyond all doubt—those of Whitney Houston. At first I thought, "She must be lip-synching." But no, this was live. For nearly an hour we were treated to a rousing Whitney Houston concert. Then the singer lit into an Indonesian ballad, every trace of American pop replaced by the quivering micro-tones of Java.

Much of big-city Java is like that singer. At first you see only the modern skyscrapers, seemingly lifted from Houston or Atlanta and deposited on Jalan Sudirman in

the middle of Jakarta. You notice the traffic and the smog, and think you could be in Los Angeles. You drive by Planet Hollywood and McDonald's. Then something completely different, something completely Indonesian makes itself known. It might be the aroma of chicken satay grilling over a coconut-husk fire, or the sight of a *becak* driver transporting five cages filled with roosters, or the sound of *gamelan* music coming from a cheap cassette player.

For more than a thousand years Java has been an international hub, a thriving trading place where East and West, south Asia and southeast Asia, India and Arabia have crossed paths. Twelve hundred years ago, an Indian traveler might have been amazed to see the world's largest Buddhist monument being built in central Java. Today, the American tourist smiles on hearing Whitney Houston. But at its core Java remains Javanese.

A good place to find that old Java is at its geographic center—the area around the royal cities of Yogyakarta and Surakarta. Long considered the cultural heart of the island, Yogya (as it's usually called) and Solo (Surakarta) have impressive *kratons* (palaces) that remain hubs for the arts—*gamelan*, *wayang kulit* puppet performances, batik, and silversmithing. The *kratons* themselves are sprawling complexes facing large open squares called *alun-aluns*.

From the outside, these palaces seem a little tired and sad—cracked walls, ill-considered renovations already falling into disrepair—nothing dramatic to catch the eye. The flotsam and jetsam of modern commercial life—such as pushcarts and trinket vendors—form a visual and spiritual barrier to the *kratons*. Disappointment is the first thing one feels at seeing these royal edifices.

But go past the nine-foot-thick walls of the Yogya *kraton* and you start to get a taste of the remarkably sophisticated—but also highly stratified—culture of traditional Java. Just inside the walls stands a large *pendopo*, an open pavilion with a forest of columns holding up a *joglo* roof. This is where guests would be received, many of whom would not be allowed to go any farther inside the royal compound. Beyond this the *kraton* unfolds as a series of building clusters around numerous courtyards. The original parts of the *kraton* date from 1757, but fire and decay have taken their toll on many different pieces of the palace—requiring rebuilding efforts at various times. Always intrigued by the latest style and fashion, the sultans of Yogya tried their hands at Hindu, Buddhist, Muslim, and European architecture—with varying results. But the overall flavor of the place is Javanese: elaborately carved wood screens, teak columns, and courtyards connected by cool dark corridors and covered walkways.

Before Islam established itself in central Java early in the sixteenth century, the Majapahit rulers of the area were Hindu. So it's not surprising that Majapahit society had its own version of a caste system. To this day the Javanese language is spoken in three different forms, depending on the rank of the person speaking and that of the person being spoken to. High, middle, and low Javanese are essentially three different dialects, reminding everyone of class and social distinctions, which may have been loosened over the past couple of generations but still cast their shadows over Javanese society.

The legacy of caste may be part of what is behind the Javanese sense of etiquette. Being polite, well-mannered, attuned to tradition, and emotionally

reserved is still important here. Raising your voice and showing emotion are considered aberrant behavior. While Americans sometimes find this Javanese reserve a bit off-putting, it is a time-tested way of coping with a population density that ranks close to the highest in the world.

A low, sprawling city, Yogya is packed with life. There seem to be more *becaks* per linear foot of road here than anywhere else in Indonesia. Colorfully painted and reminiscent of carnival rides, these human-powered taxis are often the fastest way to get through traffic (and usually the most enjoyable). Driving a *becak* is to Yogya what waiting on tables is to New York or Los Angeles: it's something nearly everyone does at one time or another to earn a few rupiah. Talk to enough *becak* drivers and you'll have spoken to college students, moonlighting batik workers, musicians between *gamelan* performances, out-of-work teachers, and the urban underclass. Invariably resourceful, these hard-pedaling cabbies will borrow a motor scooter to haul you long distances, take you to their friend's batik factory, tell you where to find the best street food, and wait while

streets of varying sizes, provide different kinds of outdoor and public spaces, encourage street life, and make connections between blocks.

Kampungs have been the basic units of Javanese cities and towns for hundreds of years and as such are the living, breathing, coughing manifestations of great experience in the art of building communities. Losing them would be a real tragedy. But leaving them alone, without running water, electricity, and proper sewage handling, is not the answer either. In Yogya, a middle course has been tested. In the 1970s, on the banks of the Kali Code River—just a block away from the modern Santika Plaza Hotel (one of the city's best)—squatters took over public land that was too steep for commercial development. An ad hoc *kampung* named Kali Code grew up quickly as several dozen families built cheap houses. While some people in the city government wanted to clear the site of the illegal residents, a Catholic priest who was also a trained architect moved into the makeshift neighborhood to see if he could help out. The priest, Romo Mangun Wijaya, studied how the people built their houses and what they needed in their community. Then he provided his own architectural expertise to complement the traditional skills of the poor. He also helped organize the residents so they could reduce crime in the area and petition the city government for official recognition and basic municipal

you visit a museum or go shopping. Separating yourself from them is the difficult part, the supply of *becaks* being so much greater than the number of passengers. Take a *becak* back to your hotel at night and don't be surprised to find the same driver waiting for you there the next morning. Realizing how important your paltry fare is to these drivers comes as a shock to those of us who think nothing of dropping several times as much money on wholly unnecessary items, like a third pair of sunglasses or a funny hat that we'll never wear back home.

Central Java is rich in culture—richer than it has been in many years. After the trauma of Japanese occupation during World War II and a couple of tumultuous decades following independence in 1945, Indonesia's economy has boomed since the 1980s. Greater wealth and more tourism have brought a revival of traditional arts—especially batik and silverwork—that had fallen into neglect. Today batik designers like Ardiyanto and Amri have made their galleries in Yogya buzzing centers of art and business—adapting motifs from abroad, rejuvenating old Javanese methods, and injecting their own personal flair into their designs.

As is common in much of Asia, and indeed parts of big-city America, wealth and poverty reside cheek by jowl in Java. Old *kampungs* (neighborhoods) with narrow streets, open sewers, and makeshift wooden houses sit at the feet of glass-and-steel skyscrapers in Jakarta. Although lacking in terms of modern hygiene, these gritty neighborhoods have developed complex urban fabrics of streets, walkways, markets, and common areas that are sorely missing from the superblock projects that today's developers are hurriedly putting up. Before all the traditional *kampungs* are wiped off the face of Jakarta, it would be wise for planners, developers, and architects to learn from them how to design services. After years of effort, Kali Code became an official neighborhood.

Central Java is also home to two of the great wonders of the ancient world: the giant Buddhist stupa of Borobudur and the Hindu temples of Prambanan. Built between 778 and 850—nearly four centuries before Chartres cathedral in France and three hundred years before the temple of Angkor Wat in Cambodia—Borobudur is a megamandala, the Buddhist symbol of the universe. A rectangular base supports circular terraces dotted with smaller stupas housing stone Buddhas. The uppermost stupa is empty, representing nirvana, the ultimate stage of the Buddha's life. Along the ten terraces are sculpted panels depicting events in the Buddha's life, a stone-relief tapestry that wraps around the walls on both sides of the walkways. Surrounded by jungle and ringed by mountains recalling Chinese landscape paintings, Borobudur is one of a handful of sites in the world with a profound power to inspire awe. My favorite memory of the place was on a day when it was invaded by several schools of Muslim teenage girls, all wearing colorful head scarves. Seen from the top of the monument, the schoolgirls were clusters of colored circles—a red group here, a white one there—perfectly complementing the carved circles of the stone stupas.

No sooner had the Sailendra rulers of Java completed Borobudur in the mid-ninth century than their dynasty crumbled. Borobudur was abandoned and soon the jungle consumed it. Not until the early nineteenth century would it be discovered by westerners, who eventually helped with several preservation efforts made over the next two centuries. The most recent (and most extensive) renovation involved disassembling the entire monument stone by stone, repairing each one, rebuilding the failing foundation, installing new drainage, then piecing it all back together. This project took ten years and was completed in 1983.

About forty miles away, Prambanan represents a different chapter in Javanese history and art. The largest of an extensive network of Hindu temples built between the eighth and tenth centuries, Prambanan sits on a fertile plain of rice fields in the shadow of Mount Merapi. Prambanan itself is a complex of temples—there may have been nearly 250 originally—of which those to the gods Shiva, Brahma, and Vishnu are the

most prominent. Stone-relief panels tell stories from the great Hindu epic, the *Ramayana*. At night, the *Ramayana* ballet is performed with the temple lit up as backdrop. The tales of clashing armies, monkey warriors, and magical spells depicted in stone on the walls of the temples are brought to life on the dance floor.

On the northeast coast of Java is Surabaya, the country's second-largest city and a manic seaport jammed with boats of every description heading in every direction. The Kalimas wharf area is two kilometers long and lined with impressive *prahu* and Bugis *pinisi*, while more modern ships dock at nearby Tanjung Perak.

On one level, Surabaya is a swampy place out of a Joseph Conrad novel, teeming with restless sailors, street hustlers, shady operators, foreign adventurers, lost souls, and busy prostitutes. Infamous for its multiple red-light districts, Surabaya caters to all preferences, from the girls in the Jarak and Bangunrejo areas to the transvestites strutting along Jalan Irian Barat—good places to gather material for a short story or a screenplay. But there is another Surabaya, one that boasts great neighborhoods of Dutch colonial buildings, broad streets lined with red-tiled houses, and dense Chinatowns where you can get goods from around the globe and some of the best Chinese food in Java.

On the other side of the island, the city of Bandung is the intellectual heart of the country. Home to nearly fifty universities—including the Bandung Institute of Technology, the country's most prestigious school for engineers and architects—it is part college town, part colonial hill station, and part industrial center. Higher, drier, and cooler than Jakarta, which is about 120 miles

to the northwest, Bandung was a favorite place for the Dutch to retreat to during hot months. In fact, the colonial authorities had drawn up plans to move the capital to Bandung in the 1930s to avail themselves of the better climate year round. A host of Art Deco hotels and buildings were erected downtown in the 1920s and 1930s, and landmarks such as the Savoy Homann and the Grand Preanger are still the best hotels in town.

Bandung is also an arts center. Some of the country's top artists are based here, supplementing their incomes with teaching jobs at local institutes and enjoying a less frantic pace than their colleagues in Jakarta. Separating the two cities is beautiful hill country with green waves of tea plantations rolling over the land.

Java is a place where new and old, modern and tra-

ditional are locked in a strange embrace that sometimes resembles a wrestling match and sometimes a tango. In this kind of relationship movement is constant, favoring one side now and the other an instant later. It has been this way for hundreds of years. When Hinduism swept through the island in the ninth century, the Sailendra dynasty crumbled and a new set of ideas, myths, and practices reverberated throughout Javanese society. Six hundred years later, the political and cultural landscape shook once again as Islam took hold. Today the pace of change is more rapid than ever, as powerful streams of foreign capital and global ideas bring with them skyscrapers and MTV. While multinational corporations are investing in operations throughout Indonesia and foreign brands such as Marlboro, Fanta, and Sony can be found in even the most out-of-the-way islands, Java is ground zero for this international invasion. The political and economic engine of the country, Java is where nearly everything starts in Indonesia.

When the people at Sun Microsystems developed a new computer language for their Web browser a few years ago, they named it Java. I don't know how they came up with this, but I think it has something to do with the magic the island still conjures in the minds of people around the world. Maybe it's the coffee connection, endless cups of Java having kept the Sun com-

puter gurus going during all those nights of writing code. Whatever the reason, the company's usurpation of the island's name can be seen as a metaphor for what is happening with the original Java. Travel from Jakarta to volcanic Mount Merapi, or from a shopping mall to the bird market in Yogya, and you'll find modernity grafted onto tradition: the hip-and-cool digital magic blending with the ancient spiritual kind. There's the old woman wearing a Muslim head scarf talking into a snazzy-looking mobile phone and the batik designer selling his wares over the Internet. There's the stockbroker who drives a BMW and plays in a *gamelan* orchestra on weekends. It's a precarious pairing that can be tacky, surprising, and inspired—sometimes all at once.

Born in Yogyakarta, the son of a banker who became a diplomat, Jaya Ibrahim lived in Singapore for several years as a child, then earned a degree in economics in England. Realizing quickly that he wasn't cut out to be a banker, Ibrahim worked as an interior designer in London during the 1980s, helping to decorate upscale houses and hotels. In 1992 he returned to Indonesia, having absorbed a heady mix of international influences but still connected in spirit to the design traditions of his homeland. "When I lived in London, I really felt it was home," recalls Ibrahim. "But in 1991 I went back to Yogya and visited the *kraton.* I realized that the architectural models I was looking for were all here in Indonesia."

A few years earlier, while still living in England, Ibrahim designed a house for his parents in Cinere, a distant suburb of Jakarta. At first glance, the house is a romantic version of Dutch colonial architecture with a few nods to the neoclassical designs of Sir Edwin Lutyens, the English architect who designed some of the key government buildings in New Delhi. A closer look shows the influence of Frank Lloyd Wright in the overhanging eaves and horizontal thrust of the house into the landscape. The interiors of the house, with

their collections of eighteenth- and nineteenth-century English prints (all set in identical wood frames), seem to reinforce the neoclassical pedigree of the design.

But behind the European surface are some uniquely Indonesian ideas at play. "The essence of Indonesian architecture is in the succession of spaces," explains Ibrahim. "How you get from the front veranda to the

inner sanctum is what Indonesian design is all about."

In Javanese design, entrances are never direct, but involve a jog or a quick turn, so evil spirits can't come in. "You're aware of the main axes of a place, but you always enter off-center," says Ibrahim. So it is with the Cinere house, completed in 1987. The main public rooms unfold as a procession of linked spaces, and an elegant gallery lined with built-in cabinets and shelves underlines the axial nature of the floor plan. But a subtle asymmetry reigns in the placement of entrances and the crossing of the house's two main axes.

Most of the furniture, all of which is made of teak, was designed by Ibrahim. Artwork and furnishings come from around the globe—celadon pots from Suma-tra, baskets from Lombok, textiles from India, brass plates from Thailand. Tying everything together is a sense of proportion that balances tall narrow windows and doors with the horizontal thrust created by long rows of framed prints and bands of small rectangular ventilation holes that run along the tops of walls and work as cornices.

A few years ago Mary Jane and Mark Edleson, Americans living in Jakarta, visited the house and fell in love with it. Mary Jane, a marketing consultant, and Mark, a top executive for Amanresorts, decided to buy the house—and everything inside it. Understanding that the artwork, furnishings, and architecture belong together, Ibrahim's mother agreed to sell it all as one.

An hour-and-a-half drive outside the clogged streets of Jakarta, beyond the rapidly developing suburbs and into the verdant hills south of the capital, Tapos is a world apart. It is here that the ceramist F. Widayanto retreats for several days each week. The Ci Hearang River runs here, feeding canals that once irrigated rice fields and supplying a reassuring gurgle that is the background music to this rolling terrain. Farther up the hill, former President Suharto has his own manicured "farm."

"I love the water, the mountainside, the plants, and the animals," says Widayanto, explaining what attracted him to the eleven-thousand-square-meter property. Although his primary residence is in Jakarta, he has spent much of his time in the Tapos area since 1983.

Working with architect Toga Panjaitan, Widayanto built this small house in 1990, designing it so it has about as much space outdoors as it does inside. Porches

and a covered dining pavilion offer wonderful places to relax and catch the mountain breezes that make the area much cooler than the sweltering capital. A bedroom for Widayanto and one for a guest are the only sleeping accommodations. A few living areas and a kitchen round out the indoor spaces.

The house is casually modern in style and built of painted concrete block. But since it incorporates such traditional elements as a sharply pitched wood-frame roof, split-bamboo blinds that can roll down and protect the wraparound veranda from sun and rain, and tropical landscaping, the house has the feeling of a building that belongs exactly where it is.

Like traditional Javanese houses, this one is essentially one floor with a mezzanine inserted under the highest portion of the roof. But the way it organizes the living spaces is clearly modern—they are arranged in a

series of rooms that open onto each other, stepping up the hillside site. Designed for a bachelor who spends much time alone but also entertains, the house is not like those built for a typical Indonesian family. Large casement windows are also unusual for the tropics, where a common design strategy is to limit the amount of hot sunlight that comes inside. But because this house is set against the side of a hill, which provides plenty of shade for much of the day, the architect could open the living spaces to views by using generous windows.

Most of the interior surfaces are painted white to provide a backdrop for the richly colored, carved, and textured furnishings. Large tropical plants, boldly patterned fabrics, all sorts of sculptures, paintings, and wooden cabinets supply plenty of stimulation for the eye. Intense color is used for just a few vertical surfaces—a rich papaya for a wall on one side of the dining area and a brilliant curry yellow in the small foyer between the indoor kitchen and the outdoor dining pavilion, where a demonic Barong carved from a giant tree root dominates the space.

A short walk along a garden path leads to a concrete-block studio where workers throw, decorate, and fire the pottery Widayanto designs. With living and work space here in Tapos, Widayanto has everything he truly needs.

SUNDA KELAPA OLD PORT, JAKARTA

This is where Jakarta began. Even today the past is visible: more than a hundred wooden *pinisi* schooners docked at an angle to the long pier, agile laborers carrying thirty-kilo bags of rice and stacks of lumber on their shoulders as they walk narrow planks from the ships to the pier, dark-skinned old women wearing conical straw hats and selling food from baskets, the buzz of maritime trade everywhere.

On the northern edge of Jakarta, where the area called Kota reaches the Java Sea, Sunda Kelapa has been a thriving port since the twelfth century. Sunda is the westernmost region of Java and *kelapa* means coconut, which was probably one of the earliest cargoes to be shipped from here. Now all kinds of goods are piled onto the wharf: early in the morning it is usually fish and seafood, later in the day lumber and dry goods.

The *pinisi* are beautiful ships, about 120 feet long and usually set with a ketch rig of seven sails. Most are made using only handsaws and traditional tools, and the older ones have hulls that are made with pegs of ironwood instead of nails and bolts. While modern freighters have taken over most international routes, *pinisi* still ply the waters throughout the Indonesian archipelago. Most can sail from Jakarta to southwest Borneo in four days and to Irian Jaya in seven. Many things have changed in Indonesia in recent years, but the country still has one of the largest fleets of sailing vessels in the world.

BOROBUDUR, CENTRAL JAVA

One of the great structures of the world, Borobudur is a monument to both political and spiritual power. Built during the height of the Sailendra dynasty, which ruled central Java from the mid-eighth to the tenth century, Borobudur is an impressive demonstration of an ancient government's ability to harness the wealth of its agricultural economy and organize a massive construction effort that took more than fifty years, ending around 824. It is also the largest Buddhist monument in the world, a triumph of religious devotion.

Approximately thirty miles northwest of Yogyakarta, Borobudur stands in a fertile valley between the Progo and Elo rivers, a location that was probably selected to evoke the confluence of the holy Ganges and Jumna rivers in India. With the towering forms of three volcanoes—Merapi, Sumbing, and Merbabu—surrounding the site and Tidar Hill (the "Nail of Java" at the geographic center of the island) nearby, Borobudur enjoys a setting of unusual power and significance.

About 115 feet high, Borobudur is a series of nine terraces rising from a platform or "foot," which was long hidden from view. The terraces are organized into three groups, each one representing a key step in a Buddhist's path to enlightenment, and are encrusted with 1,500 stone-relief panels depicting the life of the Buddha and various Sanskrit texts. Panels on the lowest levels show the "sphere of desire" (Kamadhatu), while those just above represent the "sphere of form" (Rupadhatu), a transitional realm in which humans are released from their worldly form. The highest levels are circular terraces studded with bell-shaped stupas and represent the "sphere of formlessness" (Arupadhatu) or nirvana. Originally each of the perforated stone stupas enclosed a seated Buddha, but today some of these sculptures are missing. The largest stupa, at the pinnacle of the monument, is also empty, but was probably meant to be this way since it represents the end of earthly existence, the end of a person's cycle of death and reincarnation.

Many aspects of Borobudur are still open to different interpretations. Its name, for example, is variously explained as coming from the Sanskrit words *Vhara Buddha Uhr,* meaning "Buddhist monastery on the hill," or as a variation on the words *boro* (monastery) and *budur* (a place name). The hidden foot, or foundation, is also the subject of debate: one group of experts claims it was added shortly after the monument was completed as a way of reinforcing a structure that was already showing dangerous signs of slippage; another hypothesis is that this lowest level was a part of the original design but was covered to keep its relief panels depicting earthly desire hidden from devout monks. What is beyond doubt is Borobudur's enduring ability to inspire awe.

BIRD MARKET, YOGYAKARTA

A forest of stalls stacked with cages for all kinds of creatures, the Pasar Ngasem (bird market) is not just a sprawling indoor-outdoor pet store. It is a window onto the Javanese soul, which is stirred by the music of songbirds. Turtle doves, zebra doves, spotted-necked doves, and a rainbow of other songbirds are prized by the Javanese and lavished with care. Less well attended to are larger animals, including furry cus-cus, rabbits, ducks, and monkeys—all of which can be bought at the market. If you look carefully or ask around, you can also find a few at-risk species, such as rare jungle birds and large monitor lizards.

WAYANG KULIT

Shadow plays featuring finely detailed puppets manipulated by a single master (*dalang*) have been popular in Java since at least the eleventh century. Made of stiff pieces of leather that have been elaborately carved and painted, the puppets are attached to rods of horn and have movable limbs. Performances start and end with the *gunungan* (tree of life; opposite page, bottom left) alone on the cloth screen and often continue for hours as the seated *dalang* handles all of the puppets, provides the voices and narration, and conducts the *gamelan* orchestra using a small cymbal clasped between the toes of one foot.

There is an air of exile about the colonial-style house where Guruh Sukarno lives, even though it sits near the center of Jakarta in the affluent Kebayoran Baru neighborhood. This is where his family moved after his father, the first president of Indonesia, died in 1967. Designed by Guruh's mother, Fatmawati, in 1953 and used by her as a retreat from all the political (and personal) machinations of the palace, the house is a quiet oasis surrounded by lawns and gardens.

Today its plaster walls are chipped, and the entire place needs a good paint job. Old furniture taken from the presidential palace shares floor space with rickety chairs and new pieces designed by Guruh. Framed photographs of President Sukarno with John F. Kennedy, Nikita Khrushchev, Jawaharlal Nehru, and other world leaders sit on a wooden desk in the same room as a large couch strewn with the daily newspaper and

several months' worth of magazines from around the world. A faded nobility mixes with the smell of tonight's dinner and clove-cigarette smoke.

Guruh Sukarno is a painter. His canvases of Balinese dancers, portraits of friends, and scenes of everyday Jakarta show a keen eye for expressive detail and gesture. One room of the house is used as a gallery, but paintings are in various places—leaning up against a wall here and hung from another there. Unfinished work is scattered all about, giving the rambling, high-ceiling house the feeling of a Soho loft exposed to the tropical sun.

In his forties, Guruh bears a striking resemblance to his father (who reportedly also demonstrated a talent for painting). Although he served for a time as a senator, the soft-spoken bachelor exhibits little taste for politics—a field of endeavor in which he seems happy to

let his sister Megawati take the lead. His passions lie elsewhere: with his painting and the many friends who drop by at all hours.

While others might feel burdened by the history, the fine pieces of china, and the neoclassical detailing that remain in the house, Guruh seems to inhabit it comfortably. It is what he grew up with. The most remarkable piece in the house is an eighteenth-century carved wooden screen from central Java that dominates one large room. Painted green with gold trim, the screen is mostly French baroque in design but has a few Javanese and Chinese flourishes. In the dining room a large and powerful seascape seems to speak of tumultuous forces beyond the control of individuals. Neither museum nor gilded cage, the house—which Guruh calls Puri Fatmawati in honor of his mother—is just home, a work in progress where coffee stains and ashtrays are as much a part of the place as faded photographs and new paintings.

It comes as no surprise to learn that Mary Ann Murphy owns a shop selling Indonesian furniture and furnishings in her hometown of New Orleans. There are enough extraordinary pieces of Asmat art, Javanese chairs, and Sumatran textiles in her house in Jakarta to easily supply a retail outlet or two. "I have way too many chairs," says Murphy, pointing to a set of six wood-and-rattan *kursimalas* (a type of chaise longue) that Dutch plantation owners in Java would stretch out in, their feet resting on wooden supports that swing into place. "I keep saying, 'That's the last one.' Then I find another." It's easy to see how these remarkably comfortable and beautiful items would be hard to resist.

Mary Ann and her husband, Paul, moved into this two-story contemporary house six years ago, just as it was being completed. The house itself is a conventional Western-style structure that isn't what the Murphys would have built if they had designed it themselves. But the wide-ranging collection of art and furniture in the house reveals the Murphys' knowledge and love of Indonesian design.

Much of the artwork comes from the Asmat area of Irian Jaya, where Paul's employer, Freeport Indonesia, mines for gold and other metals. Freeport's mining operations and their impact on the land are not without controversy. But the Murphys have used their frequent visits to Irian Jaya to develop a rich appreciation for the Asmat people and their culture.

In their double-height living room, the Murphys have placed two tall ancestor poles and several carved-wood shields from Irian Jaya. For each of the last five years, Mary Ann has attended a large auction of Asmat art held every October in Timika, an event that has encouraged local tribes to rediscover their artistic traditions and provided them with a steady source of

income. Mary Ann rarely leaves the auction empty-handed. Some of her finds—including spears, shields, and an eighteen-foot-long Asmat canoe—are kept in a gallery off the entry to the Jakarta house.

Not everything in the house is old or native, though. In the living room, for example, is a sculpture by Judy Emery, an American artist living in Jakarta who takes old bird cages and unravels their split bamboo or wood pieces so they become tensile works of art open to a variety of interpretations. Gesturing to the living room, Mary Ann explains, "Once you start collecting, it's hard to stop."

KALI CODE RIVER COMMUNITY, YOGYAKARTA

Just a hundred yards from one of Yogyakarta's best hotels, behind a large billboard for Bank Indonesia telling people to save for their children's education, a community of bamboo houses tumbles down the steep embankment to the Kali Code River. Begun in the 1970s as an illegal squatter settlement, the community called Kali Code (pronounced "kal-ley cho-day") has a complex history that says much about the state of politics, urban development, and relations between social classes in Java today.

Built on public land that was too steep for traditional development, Kali Code drew the attention of government officials, who wanted to tear it down, and social activists, who wanted to upgrade it into an officially recognized neighborhood with basic city services. In 1981 Romo Mangun Wijaya, a local Catholic priest who is also a trained architect, moved to Kali Code to help the residents build sturdier and more attractive houses and to organize the people into a functioning community, adding his architectural expertise to their traditional skills. For six years Romo Mangun lived at Kali Code, helping its residents erect a community hall, a few blocks of two-story apartments, and numerous single-family houses. Using simple construction methods and inexpensive materials (bamboo, coconut wood, and woven bamboo mats, for example), the residents, along with skilled carpenters, built houses that would be easy to repair and maintain. Romo Mangun also helped lay the political foundation for Kali Code to be recognized as a legal community. More important than any of the physical structures was the social organization that grew out of the people working together.

Today 35 people in 41 houses function as a single community, with security and basic sanitation provided by the group. With government recognition has come a communal water pump and hookup to the city's electrical grid. Crime is down, though

progress hasn't changed certain things. People still bathe in the polluted river at the foot of the community and sanitation is an iffy proposition. The residents—many of whom collect, sort, and then sell garbage, or work as *becak* drivers—are still uniformly poor. No one has any money to save for the education of children, as the nearby billboard exhorts. But most people here appreciate what they have. For example, Bahran Affandi, a twenty-six-year-old resident who works at one of the tire-repair shops on the street above Kali Code, says, "It's a good place to live. People come from many different places—Solo, Salatiga, Magelang—but we all get along."

PRAMBANAN, CENTRAL JAVA

At the same time as the Buddhist rulers of the Sailendra dynasty were running the show on the southern part of central Java, the Sanjayas were building a Hindu empire just to the north. The Sanjayas were traders, controlling the important Strait of Melaka and therefore much of the commerce with the spice-rich Moluccas Islands to the east.

Not to be outdone by the Sailendra dynasty's Buddhist monument of Borobudur, the Sanjaya rulers built an impressive complex of Hindu temples on the Prambanan Plain during the eighth, ninth, and tenth centuries. While there are hundreds of temples scattered over the Prambanan Plain, the largest and most important ones are a trio sharing a stone platform and commonly referred to as Candi (pronounced "chandee") Prambanan. The much smaller surrounding temples are mostly in ruins.

Set within a square court, the three main temples and five subsidiary ones represent the flowering of Hindu art in central Java. The tapestry of stone-relief panels and the multitiered buildings they wrap around are sophisticated expressions of the Hindu cosmos, in which the gods Shiva (the destroyer), Brahma (the creator), and Vishnu (the preserver) rule supreme. Not surprisingly, the three main temples at Prambanan are dedicated to this godly triumvirate.

Relief panels around the base of Candi Shiva (the largest) and Candi Brahma tell stories from the *Ramayana* epic, while those decorating Candi Vishnu depict tales of Lord Krishna from the *Mahabharata.* The temples to Brahma and Vishnu each have one chamber in its center with a sculpture of its presiding deity. The Shiva temple has four main rooms inside with sculptures of a four-armed Shiva, the sage Agastya, the elephant-headed Ganesha (Shiva's son), and Shiva's wife, Durga. Some locals say the sculpture of Durga is actually of Loro Jonggrang, "the Slender Virgin" who refused to marry an ogre and was turned to stone as punishment.

BATIK

Considered one of the high arts of Java, batik is an ancient resist-dye technique for decorating woven cloth. Traditionally, wax is poured onto the cloth using a *canting* (pronounced "chanting"), a small copper cup with a spout and a wood handle. The cloth is then dropped into dye. When the wax is melted off, the areas under it remain undyed, while the rest is colored. If a second color is desired, the process is repeated. Today few batik artists use a *canting*, relying instead on either a brush or a stamp called a *cap* (pronounced "chap") made of copper or wood.

JAKARTA SLUMS

In the shadow of modern high-rises and adjacent to the old port of Sunda Kelapa, a slum sprawls along the water. Rickety houses built of salvaged wood and corrugated metal sit on stilts above the muddy plain. Children play tag in the narrow alleys and on the wooden walkways between the houses. Someone takes a makeshift bath from a bucket of polluted water. Some of the residents work at the nearby fish market, others do manual labor wherever they can find it. Most earn at least some of their incomes from rummaging through the great mounds of garbage here, selling the few items they might find of any value.

The setting is pure suburbia: large Western-style houses line wide curving streets and cul-de-sacs, gated communities rise up from the flat featureless landscape, and nothing is older than the last building boom. So the crisp modern design and splashes of color at Burhan Tjakra's house come as a wonderful surprise, a breath of fresh air in a part of north Jakarta that was once a swampy industrial slum.

Tjakra, a young architect who runs a small firm called Datum Architecture, was educated in the United States at the University of Southern California and the University of California, Los Angeles, and returned to Indonesia in the early 1990s. While he brought back an appreciation of the fragmented forms of southern Californian architects, such as Frank Gehry and Franklin Israel, he has coupled it with an understanding of energy-efficient design and local materials.

The 3,800-square-foot house he designed for his family of four incorporates many of the ideas driving his architecture. The concrete-frame structure is frankly modern, but the massing of its forms doesn't overwhelm its more conventional neighbors. Inside the house Tjakra used mostly Indonesian materials—from Palimanan limestone pavers and granito tiles, made of ceramic and local granite powder, to wooden shutters and a strip of smooth pebbles used along one edge of the entry foyer.

All of the public rooms of the house are naturally ventilated; only the bedrooms are air-conditioned. "This is probably the only new house in this part of town that relies on natural ventilation," notes Tjakra. To cut down further on energy consumption, the architect brought in plenty of daylight through skylights and windows. "We never turn on the lights until after six," Tjakra says.

As Indonesian houses have done throughout the ages, this one weaves together indoors and out, so there seems to be no clear separation between the two

realms. Materials such as slate and pebbles that are typically used outdoors are brought inside. Daylight floods rooms from above and from all sides. Corner windows and most of the back wall of the ground floor fold away to extend the living space outdoors. Without imitating any traditional forms, Tjakra has imbued his house with the spirit of old tropical architecture. In the end, he got the best of both old and new.

Sunaryo, one of Indonesia's leading artists, likes to combine wood, stone, and metal in his abstract sculptures. Rather than expressing contrasts in materials, his work tends to blend them, showing how the human-made and technological can emerge from the natural. Sunaryo's sculptures, which help anchor the outdoor spaces around his house, can be seen as metaphors for the house itself—a sophisticated merging of elements drawn from sources as disparate as Java and Japan, Indonesia and America.

A professor at the Bandung Technical Institute, Sunaryo designed most of the house himself, with help from architect Sunpendi. In plan, the house is a simple square divided into nine parts—a scheme that recalls ancient Indian mandalas. Structurally, it is a wood-frame building with plaster walls and a ceramic-tile roof.

Just entering the house is a wonderful experience that seems to take the visitor far away from the bustling streets of Bandung. The downward-sloping driveway leads to a small, but complex, Japanese-inspired garden that combines clusters of bamboo with an array of local plantings, a shallow pool with water lilies, and a path that changes from brick to volcanic stone, dirt, then camphor-wood steps. A graceful stele sculpted by Sunaryo from mahogany and steel stands as a enigmatic sentinel in this rich landscape. The path eventually leads to a central veranda that is the dominant feature of the house's exterior.

Sunaryo, who grew up in central Java, remembers the traditional *pendopos* where people would greet their guests before entering the house proper. Covered but not enclosed by walls, Sunaryo's veranda blends colonial influences with local ones, resulting in a cross-cultural setting that is a perfect place to take tea, visit, or discuss art. A stained-glass frieze running just below the roof incorporates some glass from France, while furniture includes two curved wooden seats from Bali, a deep sitting platform from Java, and a carved-wood bridal chest from the island of Madura. Inside the house, two small sitting areas flank the front door, but

people tend to congregate in the comfortable sunken living room with its built-in banquettes covered with colorful cushions and throw pillows.

While the measurements of the house are generally based on the metric system, Sunaryo adjusted the length of walls and the height of ceilings to the dimensions of his own body. With an artist's trained eye and a sixth sense for what feels right, he made the house fit the human form, rather than vice versa. A Zen-like spiral staircase with wooden steps and no railing leads to a mezzanine.

The bedrooms are tucked off to one side of the living areas, while the dining room and kitchen are in the rear of the house to take advantage of wonderful views of rolling hills and a valley. When Sunaryo and his family moved here fourteen years ago, the view was of plantations and jungle. Today, the sound of bulldozers trumpets the arrival of new houses and suburban development.

SENDONG SONO, CENTRAL JAVA

Set in and around a small mountain ravine not far from Borobudur, Sendong Sono is a Catholic shrine where water, sky, and trees are as important to the architectural effect as the concrete block, bamboo, and wood used to build the small pavilions rambling over the site. Designed by priest-architect Romo Mangun Wijaya, the shrine weaves the built and the natural into a seamless whole.

Sendong means "source of water" and sono is "jungle," and the heart of the place is indeed a stream surrounded by thick forest. To get there you must walk a mile-long dirt path that climbs a steep hill and is dotted with little shrines commemorating the stations of the cross—the spots where Christ fell on his way to his crucifixion. At the top of the hill, you descend into a ravine terraced with octagonal concrete blocks and crossed by two footbridges. Wooden A-frame structures and pavilions with traditional Javanese *joglo* roofs offer a variety of places to pray. In May and October, thousands of Catholic pilgrims fill the entire site, turning the ravine into one large outdoor church.

Construction of Sendong Sono began in 1974 and small buildings are still being added. In designing the place, Romo Mangun says he was inspired by terraced rice fields and amphitheaters—a combination of Eastern and Western sources, which can be interpreted as a metaphor for the Catholic church in Indonesia. As in all of his architecture, Romo Mangun uses only humble materials, such as bamboo, various kinds of local wood, and prefabricated concrete. "But these materials are only dead things, so you must build an atmosphere of worship for them," explains the priest. At Sendong Sono, the landscaping, the buildings, and the ravine come alive with prayer.

YOGYAKARTA KRATON, YOGYAKARTA

More a small city than a palace, the Yogyakarta *kraton* is a sprawling network of courtyards, walkways, pavilions, and buildings accommodating everything from the sultan's private residence and ceremonial rooms to batik workshops, stores, mosques, schools, and houses for thousands of people who are either part of the extended royal family or affiliated with it. Walking through the *kraton* can be a disorienting experience as the regal blends with the mundane, the freshly renovated with the dilapidated, and the public with the private.

Begun in 1756 by the first sultan of Yogya, Hamengku Buwono I, the *kraton* took about forty years to build. But additions and renovations have been made ever since, as fire, time, and changing fashions have taken their toll. Like the Kasunanan Palace in nearby Surakarta, the *kraton* in Yogya fronts onto a large public green, the Alun-Alun Lor, which has two holy banyan trees at its center and serves as the city's most prominent soccer field and civic gathering spot. Past the food carts and vendors just outside the thick walls surrounding the royal district is a different realm: one where great open pavilions (*pendopo*) are held up by small forests of teak columns, courtyards lead onto one another, and royal attendants, armed with the traditional Javanese sword, the *kris,* move about dressed in traditional sarong, sash, and batik headgear.

Just inside the main entrance is a large *pendopo* called the Pageleran, which was originally reserved for government officials waiting to meet the sultan but is today used for *gamelan* performances that are open to everyone. Beyond this is the Siti Inggil, or high ground, where new sultans are crowned. Continuing south, the visitor finally arrives at the central sector of the *kraton*— a series of stately courtyards trimmed with dark sand taken from beaches on the south coast of Java so that the Goddess of the South Seas, Nyi Loro Kidul, feels welcome.

According to legend, Nyi Loro Kidul periodically visits the *kraton* and sleeps with the sultan, uniting heaven and earth, sea and land. She even has her own bedroom in a beautiful *sentong* (ceremonial pavilion) where offerings of food are kept just in case she drops by unexpectedly.

At the heart of the kraton is the Bangsal Kencono, or Golden Pavilion, with its four teak columns incorporating motifs representing the three religions of Java: red for Hinduism, gold for Buddhism, and black and gold for Islam. Extending beyond and around the Bangsal Kencono are residences for the various wives and children of the sultan, a *pendopo* used for *wayung kulit* performances, the royal dining room, and rooms used as museum space today.

The current sultan is a powerful figure in national as well as local politics and a great patron of Javanese arts. As a result, the Yogya *kraton* is once again a center for *gamelan, wayung kulit,* batik, silversmithing, and other traditional arts—a role it has performed periodically during its two-and-a-half-century history.

After living in places like Cambridge, Massachusetts, and Princeton, New Jersey, Arief and Leila Budiman wanted a house that brought them back in touch with their native Indonesia. So they hired Romo Mangun Wijaya, an architect and Catholic priest who is well-known for his use of local materials and his understanding of traditional building methods.

"We asked Romo Mangun for a house that is open," remembers Leila Budiman. "It was 1976 and we had been away for ten years. In Cambridge and Princeton, the houses are closed off to the cold. We really missed Indonesia. We wanted a house that's open to the warmth."

What the Budimans got was a house that is open— to varying degrees—to all of the elements: the warmth, the rain, the lizards and snakes, the fragrances of the land, and the sounds of frogs, crickets, and the muezzin calling Muslims to prayer. Four pavilions organized around a central garden, the house has woven bamboo mats for walls and traditional Javanese *joglo* roofs (which sit on four columns). All four pavilions are two stories high and rest on concrete piers shaped by bamboo forms that leave a natural imprint on the human-made material.

The pavilions follow the rolling terrain, stepping up or down the hill as needed. While some architects might have flattened a portion of the site on which to build, Romo Mangun left the land as undisturbed as possible. And while most architects would have connected the pavilions with enclosed spaces, Romo Mangun kept them separate—providing only outdoor or covered walkways. "When it rains, you get wet," states Leila with a smile.

Two of the four pavilions have outdoor sitting areas on their lower floors—shaded rooms that are perfect places to enjoy the tropical setting. One of these pavilions has a living room above, while the other has a bedroom. The other pavilions house the

kitchen on the ground floor with the master bedroom above and a library downstairs with a guest room above. All parts of the house are naturally ventilated except the library, which is air-conditioned to protect the books and computer.

A popular professor at Kristen Satya Wacanna University, Arief spoke out against certain practices of the university administration and in 1994 he was dismissed from his job. Fifty-one fellow professors and almost the entire student body protested the action. Eventually, Arief accepted a position at an Australian university and the Budimans rented out their beloved house. Leila, too, is well known in Indonesia. A psychologist, she has written the "Consultasi" advice column in *Kompas*, one of the nation's largest newspapers. Sort of an Indonesian Ann Landers, Leila has answered questions from thousands of love-lorn, love-torn, emotionally troubled, socially confused people in her columns.

The materials used in the house are mostly local and all age well in a hot, moist environment: bamboo, hard marandi wood from Kalimantan, brick, and hand-made ceramic tiles painted by fingers to look like marble. The Budimans love all the bamboo in the house. But most locals associate the material with the cheap, temporary construction that poor people use. The typical middle-class family in Java dreams of a stucco-clad southern-California suburban-style house, like the ones seen in all the Indonesian soap operas. The Budimans' neighbors were frankly befuddled by their choice of building materials. "People couldn't understand why we would build such a nice big house out of bamboo," says Leila. Most of the plantings are local as well, except for some rambutan and durian trees that were brought in for their fruit.

Whether sitting in one of the covered outdoor rooms during a brief but torrential downpour or relaxing in one of the upstairs rooms with views of forest, hills, and the koi pond in the central courtyard, guests at the Budiman house enjoy a firsthand relationship with nature. Leila notes, "When we first moved here, the children saw all the lizards, frogs, and snakes and said, 'We're living in a zoo.'"

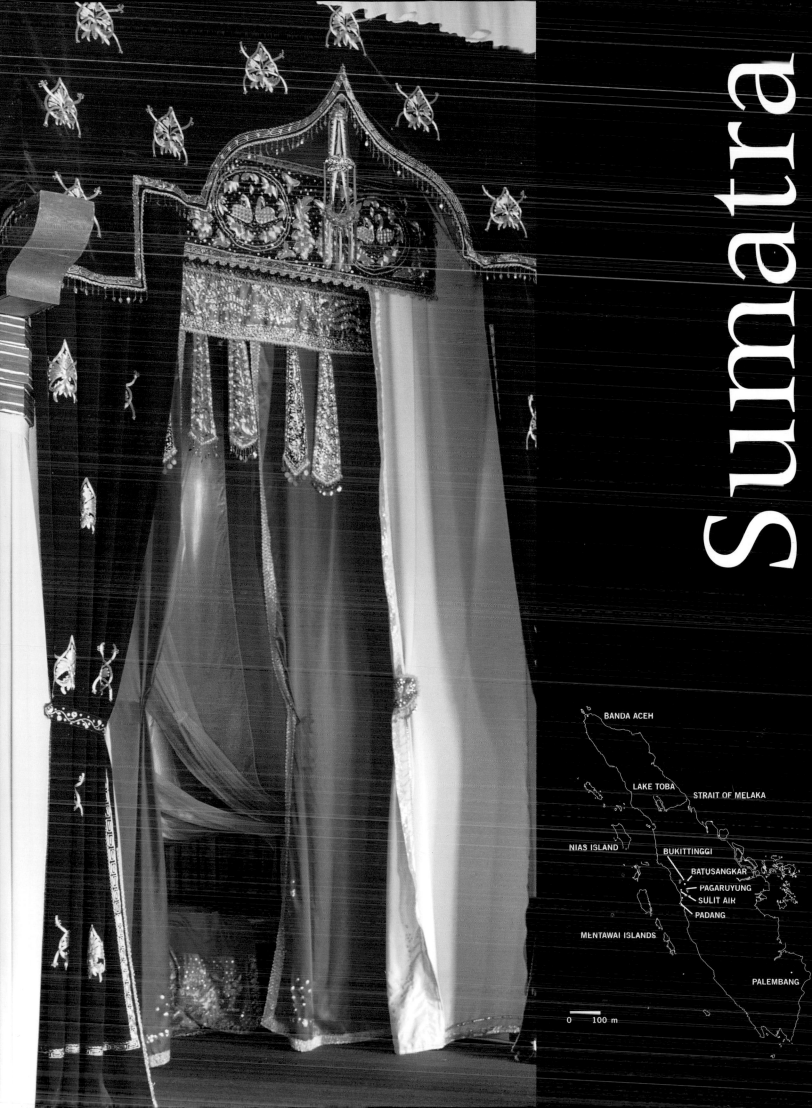

Sumatra

BANDA ACEH

LAKE TOBA
STRAIT OF MELAKA

NIAS ISLAND
BUKITTINGGI
BATUSANGKAR
PAGARUYUNG
SULIT AIR
PADANG

MENTAWAI ISLANDS

PALEMBANG

0   100 m

It may be called the "Isle of Gold," but today it is black gold—oil—that brings in the big money. Add to this the island's highly prized coffee, pepper, rubber, and palm plantations, and rich deposits of coal, bauxite, aluminum, and tin, and it is obvious why Sumatra is such an important part of the Indonesian economy. The sixth-largest island in the world, Sumatra accounts for a quarter of Indonesia's entire land mass. But the island has a population density of just thirty-three people per square kilometer, compared with Java's nine hundred.

When it comes to animals, no Indonesian island tops Sumatra. The diversity of fauna is mind-boggling: 176 species of mammals, 194 reptiles, 62 amphibians, and 520 birds. Orangutans—the so-called people (*orang*) of the forest (*utan*)—live in the north along with the few remaining Sumatran rhinoceroses and wild pigs. The island is also famous for its tigers, which the locals address as "grandfather" when they cross paths, and its elephants, which are smaller (just six feet high) and less hairy than their African cousins. If that is not enough, there are also the Sumatran clouded leopards, sun bears, honey bears (which can walk upright on their hind legs), goat antelopes, pigtailed macaques, and large-nosed proboscis monkeys.

Sumatra's mangrove forests are equally rich in biodiversity, with trees like the ketapang that reach 180 feet. There are also a number of flowering freaks, such as the corpse plant, which has the aroma of a decaying animal carcass, and the Goliath of the bloom world, the

rafflesia. Named after Sir Thomas Stamford Raffles, who was Britain's lieutenant governor in Sumatra from 1818 to 1823, the rafflesia grows along the island's west coast. Raffles was a noted botanist (and a founder of the Zoological Society of London) who called the three-foot-wide blooms the biggest flowers in the world, which is half right, since the plant is actually a fungus (not a flower) that grows on the forest floor and explodes once a year with orange petals decorated with white spots. Like the corpse plant, the rafflesia lets loose a major stink when it blooms.

Alas, Sumatra's great forests are disappearing at an alarming clip. Logging and slash-and-burn farming are the main culprits. According to satellite analysis, nearly 30 percent of the island's forest was destroyed from 1982 to 1990. In the dry season, smoke is in the air everywhere, and in 1997 major forest fires affected air traffic over Sumatra, the Strait of Melaka, and Malaysia.

Having read news stories of the logging, mining, and oil production in Sumatra, I had envisioned a

mutant hybrid of Kentucky, the Amazon, and Kuwait. I wasn't prepared for the eye-popping beauty of the landscape: rugged volcanoes, crater lakes, terraced fields of rice, thick jungle. Bali might have more exquisitely sculpted rice paddies and Java has equally impressive volcanoes, but Sumatra's landscape has a sense of wildness to it that has been lost on the more populated islands of Indonesia. Even in the large cities, such as Palembang (population 700,000) and Padang (population 500,000), there remains a frontier feeling that nature has taken a good beating but has not yet been defeated. Go just a few kilometers beyond the cities and you can feel the hot breath of the jungle all around you.

Sumatra somehow feels more Islamic than most other parts of Indonesia. In central Java I saw more women wearing Islamic headdresses, and in Jakarta I saw larger mosques with more worshippers. But perhaps because the density of people and buildings is much lower in Sumatra, the Islamic elements stand out more powerfully. The scratchy sound of the muezzin booming forth from a small mosque's old loudspeaker

struck me more deeply one evening in a village between Bukittinggi and Batusangkar than anywhere else in the archipelago. It seemed to go to the core of this place. Indeed, Islam got its first Indonesian foothold in north Sumatra around present-day Banda Aceh before the thirteenth century. To this day, Banda Aceh is a fiercely Muslim area, proud of its history as the starting point of the Islamic wave that eventually swept over the entire archipelago.

As early as the sixth century, Sumatra was the most powerful island in the region, controlling the Strait of Melaka and the key trading routes from Arabia and India to east Asia. In the seventh century, the seafaring Srivijaya empire, based in Palembang on the east coast, ruled Sumatra, west Java, and parts of Malaysia, and had commercial influence that stretched all the way to the island of Formosa (Taiwan).

Today Palembang is still a major trading port and a center of the Indonesian oil industry. Not known for its beauty, it sprawls along the wide and muddy Musi River: great expanses of rickety wooden houses perched on tall stilts to accommodate rising waters. The traditional house (*rumah lima*) is built in the Malay

fashion with a front veranda and various parts set at different levels (usually a step or two apart). The bedroom in the center of the plan is on the highest level. Kitchens are often in separate structures in the rear or to one side. Since the river is the city's great artery, most houses face it and are reached by wooden pathways raised on piles over the water. Some of these raised paths are quite long, requiring residents to walk on narrow planks with no railing, often loaded down with water buckets and groceries. The river is an all-purpose feature, serving as road, bath, toilet, laundry, and swimming pool. Small boats equipped with noisy

outboard engines zip up and down the river, pounding through the wakes of larger ships carrying lumber and dry goods to market. It is not a pretty scene, but it is certainly lively.

All along the eastern coast of Sumatra, from Palembang in the south to Banda Aceh in the north, the Malay influence is strong—reflecting geographic prox-

imity, trading patterns, and centuries of intermarriage. In Banda Aceh, traditional houses use the Malay plan with rooms at different levels and a front veranda, but are distinguished by their carved and fretted wood gables (*tolak angin* or "shield against the wind") that slope outward at about a thirty-degree angle.

In the highlands of north-central Sumatra are the Batak peoples who build some of the most remarkable houses on the island. While related to each other, the Batak fall into six different groups, with varying languages and religions. The Angkola and Mandailing in the southern part of the region are Muslim, but the Toba, Pakpak, Simalungun, and Karo are mostly Christian, having been converted by missionaries during the past 150 years. The heart of the Batak culture is the deep volcanic Lake Toba and the holy island of Pulau Samosir that sits inside it.

Because they build permanent villages and practice wet-rice cultivation, the Toba and Karo have developed the most sophisticated architecture of the Bataks. The other tribes have traditionally relied on slash-and-burn farming, which forces them to move often and doesn't give them much incentive to invest in elaborate buildings. The great saddle-shaped roofs and carved gables of the Toba

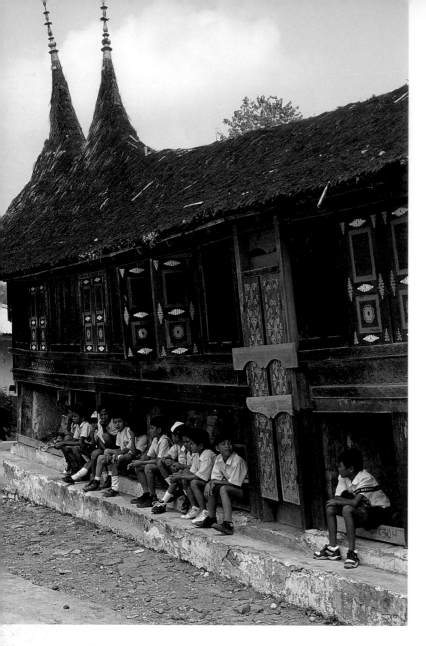

to the next customer. Typical dishes include a chewy beef (*rendang*), fried pigeon, boiled eggs, curried chicken, beef heart, chicken livers, and a variety of other innards and guts. All of it has a spicy kick. Minang men are so famous for being in the food business that a common joke explains that the first Indonesian on the moon will be an astronaut, but the second will be a Sumatran who will open a Padang restaurant.

The water buffalo is the symbol of the Minang people, inspiring the upturned roofs found on traditional buildings and playing a key role in the culture's foundation myth. According to legend, a powerful Javanese army came to Sumatra, intent on conquest. Rather than confront this superior force in a conventional way, the Minang offered a different kind of battle—between buffalo, not men. "Send out your biggest, strongest water buffalo and let him fight ours," proposed the Minang leaders to the Javanese. "If our buffalo loses, we will surrender. If yours loses, you must go home."

The Javanese accepted and on the appointed day paraded out with a truly monstrous buffalo. The Minang, on the other hand, presented a young calf, which they had starved for many days. Unbeknownst to the cocky Javanese, the Minang had strapped razor-sharp blades to the baby buffalo's horns. When the hungry calf saw the other buffalo, it mistook the adult for its mother and hurried over for some suckling. In its desperate search for milk, the calf gored the soft underbelly of the Javanese bull, killing the giant beast. At the moment of victory, the locals cried, "Minang kerbau! Minang kerbau," meaning "Victorious buffalo, victorious buffalo!"

Whether you believe that tale or not, the sweeping, multigabled roofs of the Minang do look like the long, curving horns of the local buffalo. Traditionally, these roofs were thatched with *ijuk*, a black fiber taken from the trunks of the sugar palm. Raised as much as ten feet above the ground on wood pillars, Minang houses are entered by way of a notched log that can be pulled up to keep out animals, snakes, and trespassers. Today, many of the old houses have new roofs of corrugated metal and front stairs of concrete or wood.

Batak cut dramatic figures along the shores of Lake Toba and give the pile-raised houses the look of grounded boats. The Karo build houses with a variety of roof forms—some that are pyramidal in shape and others that are hipped and sometimes topped by a second roof. Both the Toba and Karo paint the carved-wood portions and split-bamboo walls of their houses in colorful patterns.

Probably the most famous architecture of Sumatra comes from the Minangkabau (Minang) people who live in the west-central part of the island around Bukittinggi and Padang. Although Muslim, the Minang have a matrilineal structure to their society. Property is owned and inherited by the women. Untethered by real estate, the men often travel abroad on business, running trading companies and restaurants. Throughout Indonesia and much of Asia, you'll find Padang-style restaurants serving the spicy food of the Minang. This is Indonesian fast food: a dozen or more dishes are carried in on the arms of a Sumatran waiter as soon as you sit down. Whatever you eat, you pay for. Whatever you leave untouched goes back to the kitchen to be served

The *rumah gadang* (traditional house) usually has an elaborately carved wooden facade on the front, which is painted in bright colors—either a red-and-black scheme taken from Chinese design or a combination of pastels that can include blue, turquoise, white, yellow, and brown. Carved-wood pieces often drip down at least part of the way from the roof on the two sides as well. The back of the house and the lower portions of the sides, though, are made of woven split-bamboo panels.

The layout of these old houses is very simple—in front is a veranda, followed by a long open space for living and dining, and in the back are bedrooms. As in Malay architecture, the main portions of the house step up in height as you move from front to back, so the bedrooms are a few steps higher than the main living space, which is higher than the veranda. Since this is a matrilineal society, the bedrooms are for the women of the family. Husbands get visitation rights, but spend much of the time either abroad or at a separate house near the local mosque. By tradition, it is the matriarch's brother who is the handyman around the house and builds extensions at the two ends when more space is needed.

These days, few Minang live in traditional houses, and the old ways of husbands relating to wives have also loosened up quite a bit. But the upturned roof has become such an identifiable feature of Minang culture that it is used on nearly every new public building. Reduced to a kind of architectural logo and rendered in asphalt shingles and shiny metal, the Minang roof is plopped down on eight story government buildings, concrete-frame shopping centers, even public phone booths. Sometimes this comes across as endearing kitsch, slyly winking at us, as if to say, "Let's have a little fun." Sometimes, though, it degrades the original, mocking the authentic with cheap imitation.

But a visit to one of the smaller, poorer villages near Batusangkar or Payakumbuh is still a trip back in time. Old wooden houses crowd together along narrow dirt roads. Mothers open carved shutters to call out to their children, who scamper up notched-timber ladders to return home. Water buffalo still pull heavy wooden plows through the mud in flooded rice fields. And packs of mangy dogs pile into the backs of pickups on their way to help Minang men hunt for wild pigs. The rhythm and tempo of life here is ancient, even with the introduction of trucks and television. How much longer this will last is another question.

Down the road less than a mile from the royal district of Pagaruyung sits a small gem of Minangkabau architecture—a simple house that belongs to a widow named Baniah. Although it has no more than 750 square feet inside, the house proudly sports a four-pointed Minangkabau roof and an elaborately carved and painted wood facade.

Now seventy-five years old, Baniah moves slowly but gracefully around the front yard, finishing some chores before showing her house to a few guests. Inside there are just two rooms—a sitting room up front under a pointed gable and a large living space that can be divided by a curtain in the rear to create a private bedroom. The sitting room is the only part of the house with glass windows; all other windows have only wooden shutters to keep out the rain and wind.

A cabinet in the center of the main space divides it into a dining area on one side and a living room on the other. A television set has pride of place in the living area along with an octagonal wall clock, which doesn't work, and a faded calendar. A bittersweet charm fills the house, evoking the passage of time.

Baniah returns to the front yard to feed her chickens and start preparing lunch in a brick hut that serves as her kitchen. A daughter and her family live next door in a modern house that is still under construction, so Baniah is hardly alone. Two other grown children live elsewhere and return with their families during the Muslim holy month of Ramadan. Altogether there are ten grandchildren, most of whom are grown and contribute to the upkeep of the family house, the *rumah gadang*. In fact, it was the grandchildren who paid for the new carved-wood facade that was installed four years ago. Though in Minangkabau society migration is an established practice—especially for the men, who own no land—family ties are strong and a matriarchal social structure ensures that widows like Baniah remain the focus of attention.

The man of the house is eighty-one years old and has three children. No, make that eleven children. One son. Ten daughters? No, just five daughters. But that doesn't add up. Nasruddin Datuk Tan Japa, wearing a brown-and-gold batik shirt, beige slacks, and no shoes, has a quiet intensity that draws you close. You listen to his stories, never quite sure if it is the translation or the stories that seem a little off. Then you learn he has had four wives, all selected for him according to *adat* (traditional law). The different number of children are from each wife. The arithmetic starts to make sense and gets more impressive with each generation. Eleven children, forty-five grandchildren, and, so far, eighteen great-grandchildren.

The house is the Istana Silinduang Bulan, a royal palace in Pagaruyung, which Nasruddin's last wife, Putri Nur Fatimah, owned until she died in 1996 at the age of seventy-four. In Minangkabau society, it is the women who own property, although the men still wield much of the political power.

Today, no one lives at the *istana*. But as the *rumah gadang* (traditional house) for a powerful family, it is where all those children, grandchildren, and great-grandchildren converge during Ramadan and where special celebrations take place. Long ago, the local sultan would meet here with his advisers.

The original house, built in the mid-nineteenth century, burned down in 1961. The catastrophic event is seared in Nasruddin's memory: "Thursday, August 10, 1961. Eleven o'clock in the morning." Following traditional methods of construction and taking two years of work, the *istana* was rebuilt in 1987. The multipointed Minangkabau roof and elaborately carved wood facades were meticulously re-created, as were the two rows of thick wood columns and the eight sleeping alcoves around the main space inside. The Minang don't live in an orthogonal world of straight lines and right angles, so in this house the first row of six columns leans toward the front of the house and the windows slope in the same direction as the roof.

The main room of the palace is decorated in colorful fabrics—burgundy, saffron, royal blue, black, and shocking pink—that cover walls, ceiling, even the double row of columns. Although one open space, the main room steps up from front to rear in four levels—the highest one originally being reserved for the sultan and the royal family.

Out front stand two *lumbung* (rice barns) raised on tall stilts to keep rodents out. During the heyday of the Istana Silinduang Bulan, there were nine *lumbung*, manifestations of royal affluence. While the power and wealth of the royal family may have waned and delivery trucks may have made large barns obsolete, there is still some majesty left in the old house. Just ask Nasruddin.

HEADSTRONG

In the Minang highlands, as in much of Indonesia, women carry impressive loads on their heads. An expertly tied scarf or special headgear helps cushion the burden and holds everything from groceries to bundles of clothes in place. Other types of headdress are more for show, rooted in local customs and signaling the place a woman calls home.

WINNOWING RICE

A daily chore for villagers in rural Sumatra is separating rice kernels from their outer chaff. After being dried in the sun, the rice is scooped up in a shallow basket, shaken vigorously to loosen the flaky chaff, then tossed in the air and onto a large mat. When performed by an individual like this Minang woman, the task is transformed into something close to ballet.

ISTANA BASA, PAGARUYUNG

A replica of a palace that the Dutch destroyed in 1804, the Istana Basa today serves as a museum to Minangkabau culture. Built in 1976, a few kilometers from the original site, the *istana* sits on a well-groomed piece of land with freshly mowed lawns, long hedges, and a sacred mountain in the rear. Although it is supposedly a duplicate of the ancient palace, there is a theme-park feeling to the place that brings to mind Disney as much as old Sumatra.

The building is certainly big—three stories high with eight pointed Minangkabau gables sweeping across its breadth and two cross gables slicing through the center of the composition. All of the carved wood on the three main facades and the angled wood columns supporting the structure are beautifully detailed. The roof is thatched with black *juk* (more expensive than *alang-alang*), and metal finials cap each of the gable points. Several rice barns sit around the palace, symbols of status and wealth.

Behind the palace is a *surau,* a building where unmarried men and boys over seven years old would live. When in town, married men often stay at the *surau* as well. According to E. M. Loeb in his 1935 study, *Sumatra: Its History and People,* "a man neither gains possession of a woman by marriage nor a woman a man. By the payment of a certain price the woman rents the services of her husband at night. The husband then can sleep with his wife in her *bilik,* the small sleeping room of the family house, or else with the men in the men's house."

On the inside, the palace is more museum than great house. Display cases show various Minangkabau crafts and royal objects, while the colors of the decorative fabrics represent the most important towns in the area. The first floor has nine *bilik* lined up along the back of the main meeting area, while the second floor and the small third floor are now equipped with display cases as well as traditional furnishings.

About twenty-five miles southeast of Bukittinggi, the village of Sulit Air is off the tourist map, untouched by package tours and well-heeled travelers. Along narrow dirt streets, old houses—mostly in disrepair—huddle together. Small children scamper down the steps of traditional houses to greet the rare foreign visitor, occasionally asking for handouts and happily posing with each other or a water buffalo for spare change.

Set among the small single-family houses is a communal long house—stretching nearly two hundred feet along the road and raised on stilts six feet off the ground. Four sets of stairs and doors provide access. When it was built 150 years ago, the house accommodated about eight families, each with its own group of bedrooms in the rear. The great room, running the length of the structure, was common space where everyday activities and special ceremonies would take place. Now only two families live here and many of the small sleeping rooms or (bilik) are used for storage.

Thick wooden columns break up the flowing space of the great room, providing a sense of scale and a visual rhythm. While the floor is mostly bare wood planks, some areas have been covered with woven-bamboo mats and others with plastic mats. Most days, the women of the house prepare meals on portable stoves in the great room. But on feast days, the area under the house is used as a large covered kitchen and dining takes place upstairs.

Every three years all the people whose families once lived here return for Ramadan and bring the house alive. Syamsinar, the seventy-five-year-old matriarch of the house, who has lived her entire life here, says, "The house is filled with people once again. Hundreds of people. I can't count—so many!"

WORKING THE LAND

Man, woman, and buffalo share the burden of working the land in Sumatra—though the division of labor doesn't always seem fair. Plowing the muck of a flooded rice field is man's work, assisted by beast. But inserting rice plants into the mud, maintaining the paddies, and harvesting the rice is done mostly by women and children.

MARKETS

An open field, the street, the sidewalk—each can become a market at the right time. Early in the morning, an old woman makes sweet rice rolls for people to have for breakfast. Later in the day, most of the village converges on a produce market where everything from colorful shallots to great bundles of cinnamon sticks are sold. And throughout the hot afternoon, boys peddle their shaved-ice-and-sticky-syrup carts around town looking for customers.

Sulawesi

CELEBES SEA

MANADO

TALIABU ISLAND

LAKE POSO

RANTEPAO

UJUN PADANG   BONE

BUTUNG ISLAND

0   100 m

Shaped like a spider or an orchid or a cartoon crocodile (depending on your frame of mind), Sulawesi is more a collection of four narrow peninsulas joined at the hip than an island. Indeed, early European explorers thought the place was a group of islands and called them the Celebes, from the Portuguese Ponto dos Celebres (Cape of the Infamous Ones), infamous for all the shipwrecks gathered in its rugged waters. Mountainous at its center and along much of its peninsulas, Sulawesi supports a diversity of habitats for plants, animals, and people.

With 69,225 square miles of land, Sulawesi is a little smaller than Great Britain and supports 127 native species of mammals. But thanks to the rugged terrain and elongated form of the island, which separate the various habitats, more than 60 percent of the species are endemic or unique to Sulawesi. If you don't count bats, fully 98 percent of all mammal species are found only on this island—a truly remarkable figure.

Also contributing to the unusual nature of Sulawesi's nature is its position adjacent to what is known as Wallace's Line, an invisible, yet biologically important, division between the eastern and western halves of the Indonesian archipelago. Alfred Russel Wallace was the great nineteenth-century naturalist who developed—independent of, but nearly simultaneous with, Charles Darwin—the theory of evolution. What the Galápagos Islands were to Darwin, the Malay and Indonesian archipelago was to Wallace. After traveling through the region, Wallace discovered that the flora and fauna of the islands to the east of this line were related to those of Australia, while the plants and animals to the west were akin to mainland Asia. Wallace's Line runs north to south, separating Bali from Lombok and Borneo from Sulawesi, islands that are close geographically but are divided by profound differences in their natural histories.

In terms of its people, Sulawesi became famous first for its intrepid pirates, the Bugis, who would set out from the numerous protected coves on its southwest peninsula and terrorize trading ships throughout the archipelago. Sailors would tell stories of these wicked "bogeymen," a term used even today to frighten children around the world. The Bugis are still around, and, while they have (mostly) abandoned their piratical ways, they remain skilled seamen, plowing the waves

in their spectacular, handmade ships called *prahu*. These forward-tilting and square-bowed wooden boats with large rudders are remarkable pieces of design and construction—made with no plans and only simple tools. The largest examples weigh in at two hundred tons and are usually fitted out with two masts and seven rectangular sails. With a good wind a big *prahu* can sail as fast as thirty kilometers per hour.

The four main ethnic groups in Sulawesi are the Bugis and Makassarese in the southwest, the Toraja in the central highlands, and the Minahasanese in the northeast. While the Bugis and Makassarese are Mus-

lims, the Toraja and the Minahasanese are mostly Christian.

Like the Bugis, the Makassarese are great sailors and had established a powerful naval presence as early as the fourteenth century. By the seventeenth and eighteenth centuries they had gathered political clout as well, exerting control over parts of Borneo, Sumatra, and Singapore.  Makassar ships traveled throughout Asia—from China to Burma, Cambodia, the Philippines, and India. Some even ventured into the South Pacific to New Guinea and northeastern Australia. The glory days ended when the Dutch asserted control over most of Sulawesi in the nineteenth and twentieth centuries. In the Victorian era, Makassar was famous in the West for a type of greasy hair oil made from coconut that led to the development of an even more famous response: the antimacassar, a piece of fabric set on headrests and the backs of plush chairs to protect furniture from oily hair.

Today no one remembers Makassar oil, and the once-reclusive Toraja are now the island's biggest attraction. Rarely encountered by outsiders before the Dutch took control over all of Celebes in 1905 and feared as headhunters for much of their history, the Toraja have mostly converted to Christianity. Quick learners, they are becoming skilled in the art of cultural tourism.

Due to its recent arrival, Christianity here is strongly laced with local animism and ancestor worship. The old religion, called Aluk Todolo (Worship of the Spirits of Ancestors), is embraced by only a minority of Toraja today, but its rituals and beliefs are too deeply embedded in Toraja culture to just disappear. Indeed, most tourists come specifically for that old-time religion—to witness the elaborate rituals and practices distinctive to Tana Toraja (Toraja Land).

Death is a big thing here. Funerals can last a week or two and preparations for the event often take months. In the meantime, the corpse is partially embalmed, wrapped in richly patterned blankets and textiles, and kept in the family house. Traditionally, funerals would take place in fields (*rante*) where towers dedicated to ancestors stood guard. Rows of temporary buildings were erected, only to be abandoned at the

end of the ceremonies. Impressive displays of conspicuous consumption were—and still are—an important part of a person's passage from life to death, devouring large chunks of a family's wealth but establishing its status among the neighbors. Buffalo and pigs are slaughtered, hundreds of people are fed, palm wine is drunk in large quantities, dance and song are performed, and all sorts of fights are staged—from cocks to buffalo to kick boxers. Not too long ago, it was customary for the Toraja to make a human sacrifice at the funeral of an important person. Nowadays, a buffalo is used instead.

When the feasting is over, the corpse is brought out of the house on a stretcher shaped like a miniature rice barn and is taken to cliffs where the body is carried up a precarious bamboo ladder on the shoulders of sure-footed men and then interred in a cave carved into the rock face. Burying the dead in the sides of cliffs probably started as a way of protecting the jewelry and valuables accompanying the deceased—and the best spots, reserved for the wealthy, were those at the most inaccessible top.

Outside the caves, on balconies built onto the rock face, stand wooden effigies of the dead, which are carved, painted, and dressed in full sets of clothes. Called *tau tau,* these effigies are crowded onto their wooden galleries, standing like mute spectators at a sporting event. With the growing renown of the Toraja, these *tau tau* have become valuable art objects and have replaced the buried jewelry as the prime target of local grave robbers.

Another remarkable burial tradition is reserved for children. Instead of being interred in cliff caves, babies that die are buried inside sacred trees in holes that are sealed with small wooden doors. As time passes, the tree grows over the hole and door, leaving only a scar—a poetic reminder of a young life lost.

According to one version of the local origin myth, the Toraja came to their current homeland "from the

Pleiades in skyships." And one way of translating the Buginese word *toraja* is "people from above." Ethnically, too, the Toraja are different from their neighbors, a fact that has allowed anthropologists to develop a variety of theories. Lorne and Lawrence Blair, the English brothers who created the *Ring of Fire* book and video series about their journeys through Indonesia in the 1970s and 1980s, played up the extraterrestrial theory of Toraja origins—more for dramatic effect than out of belief, I surmise. Nevertheless, if you look long enough at the sweeping saddle-back roofs of the traditional Toraja house (*tongkonan*), it is possible to imagine the architectural memory of a spaceship.

The more sober, though less exciting, reading of the record has the word Toraja translated as "people of the high country," with their ancestors coming from Cambodia in great wooden boats. In fact, it is easier to see Toraja houses as ships sailing the seas rather than the

skies. And it is not difficult to see a resemblance to the houses of people on other Indonesian islands—particularly the Minangkabau of Sumatra—who also use saddle-back roofs.

But even the more academic take on Toraja origins can't diminish the fantastical quality of this people's art and architecture. A traditional village is a row of prow-shaped houses raised on square wood columns facing a row of similarly shaped but smaller granaries set on round columns. Houses face north with their entrances on the east, where the rising sun gives life and where the Toraja bury the placenta of their newborns.

Constructed with no nails, just perfectly crafted tongue-and-groove joints, Toraja buildings have layered bamboo roofs and walls embellished with distinctive red, black, and white carvings depicting buffalo locking horns, pigs, and traditional ceremonies. It is not unusual to find a rice barn richly decorated with a frieze showing—like a storyboard for a Hollywood movie—scene after scene of Toraja life: people dancing, pigs being carried to market, the ever-present water buffalo plowing a field or fighting a rival. The Toraja style of decoration uses a limited palette of earth tones—dominated by a rich burnt sienna and black—and strong swirling lines. There is not much depth of field in these pictures: everything is flattened into one plane.

Another group of people is the Bajau, the so-called Sea Gypsies, who once lived their entire lives on boats—sometimes never setting foot on dry land. Traders and fishermen, the Bajau would roam the coasts, never settling down in any one place. Some-

times connected to the Bugis or the Makassarese, the Bajau are probably related to a group of itinerant clans who have wandered through the waters around Borneo and eastern Sumatra for hundreds of years. Nowadays most Bajau have a more settled lifestyle on land, but a few thousand still live in boats on the Banggai Islands and around Kendari Bay in eastern Sulawesi.

Water, of course, is one of the defining features of Sulawesi. No part of the island is more than fifty-five miles from the coast, and thirteen major lakes dot the landscape. Lakes Towuti and Poso are the second- and third-largest lakes in Indonesia, while some—such as Tondano and Moat in the north—are dramatic bodies of water in the craters of ancient volcanoes.

Tucked into the center—the veritable navel—of Sulawesi, Lake Poso has always held a special place in the island's mythology. According to legend, Poso is the point around which heaven and earth revolve, and, indeed, locals say a rope—or perhaps an umbilical cord—once connected the two realms here. Formerly home to fierce tribes who would partake in occasional head-hunting, the Lake Poso area today has a more laid-back reputation as a place to enjoy a lazy boat ride or a quiet swim. And instead of contemplating one's own navel, visitors can admire that of an entire island.

For a number of years, traditional Toraja houses (*tongkonan*) seemed to be a dying breed—the old ones falling into disrepair and few new ones taking their place. In the process, the skills to build and decorate these remarkable structures were disappearing as well. Roofs of overlapping bamboo shingles were replaced with corrugated metal, thick timbers slotted together like those of a log cabin were abandoned in favor of lumber cut at factories, and wooden pegs were eliminated by easier-to-use metal nails.

One of the beneficial side effects of growing tourism in Tana Toraja is a renewed appreciation of traditional architecture. Tourists who travel all the way to the highlands of central Sulawesi don't want to see the same kind of houses that can be found in Jakarta or Houston. Prodded by capitalistic self-interest, the Toraja are rediscovering their architectural roots and learning how to make a profit from them, too.

Opened near the end of 1997, the Sesean Mountain Lodge in Rantepao offers visitors a chance to spend a night or two in an old-fashioned *tongkonan*. Although newly constructed and equipped with modern plumbing and services, the main lodge and the individual houses were built using mostly traditional materials and methods. Surrounded by gardens and rolling hills, the buildings make no attempt to re-create the traditional plan of a Toraja village (in which a row of houses faces a row of rice barns). Purists may not be satisfied, but projects such as this small hotel are helping to keep traditional construction skills alive in Tana Toraja.

Like the Toraja cosmos, the traditional house in this part of Sulawesi is divided into three parts—the great sweeping roof and projecting gables represent the realm of the gods; the central living area, the world of humankind; and the section under the raised floor, the land of the dead. Made of timbers cut so they lock together and using only wooden pegs—no nails—the *tongkonan* is as much a symbol of family and custom as it is a place to live. Home to one's ancestors and the repository of heirlooms, the *tongkonan* is cared for and its upkeep contributed to by everyone in the extended family, even those who live far away.

The most prominent feature of the house is its saddle-back roof, a powerful form that recalls the great ships in which the Toraja people came to their homeland eons ago; it also brings to mind the curving horns of water buffalo, the local signifier of power, wealth, and status. The importance of the buffalo is hard to miss—it is everywhere from the stylized horns of fighting bulls carved into wood panels to the stacks of real horns hung from the tall pole supporting the house's sloping front gable. Every house also has a realistically carved buffalo head above the front door. What is fascinating about this buffalo fixation is the way the Toraja mix the stylized with the realistic, the evocation with the actual.

The *tongkonan* always faces north, toward the life-giving realm of the gods and the direction from which the Toraja ancestors supposedly came. In traditional villages, a row of rice barns stands across the street from the row of houses. Similar in design, but smaller, the barns are echoes of the houses they face. To protect rice barns from hungry rodents, the storage areas are raised off the ground about six feet, supported on round columns that are smoothed so four-legged intruders can't climb them.

As with most Indonesian tribes, the building of a Toraja house is a sacred event, marked with various ceremonies. Before construction begins, a sacrifice must be made—usually a chicken or pig, but sometimes a buffalo, if the family is wealthy or prominent. When the house is completed, a feast takes place and many animals are slaughtered to feed all the guests.

BUILDING A BARN

Although made by hand, traditional Toraja rice barns combine on-site and pre-fabricated construction. For example, the heavy timber elements, such as thick columns and cross beams, are usually cut to size and notched with mortises in a temporary workshop off-site. Also, sections of bamboo staves are bound together with rattan and stored so they can be installed on the barn later. Meanwhile, at the construction site a bamboo scaffold is erected and the timber components are fitted together—wooden tongues in notched grooves. The roof is made of layered bamboo woven together with long strips of flattened split bamboo. Thatch or bamboo shingles will cover the roof and carved wood panels will be slid into pre-cut grooves to form walls. Finally, the wall panels will be painted in the black, orange, and white color scheme that the Toraja love.

LANDSCAPE

Water and earth. In a place where wet-rice cultivation is a primary activity, the meeting of these two elements is more than just a matter of scenery. It is the dietary and cultural foundation of society. And since the land is carefully shaped by the farmers who have worked it for centuries, the meeting of water and earth is also where nature and human endeavor converge.

TAU TAU, RANTEPAO

The Toraja's traditional religion, *Aluk Todolo*, is rooted in a careful balancing of opposites—life and death, east and west, morning and evening, white and black. With the assertion of Dutch control in the early twentieth century and the success of Christian missionaries later in the century, many of the Toraja's traditional life-oriented ceremonies (including circumcision, teeth filing, and body decoration) were discouraged. More understanding of the need for funerals, European authorities allowed the local death rituals to continue. As a result, the Toraja are now best known for their elaborate funerals and burials—rituals that the Toraja perform on a grand scale and in dramatic fashion.

The funeral effigies (*tau tau*) that are placed in caves cut into cliff faces are actually a relatively recent component of Toraja burials, having begun perhaps only in the nineteenth century. Previously, the Toraja carved wooden sarcophagi (*erong*) in the shape of houses, boats, or animals and placed them at the base of cliffs. The Buginese to the south, however, made a habit of robbing these graves of the treasures buried with the bodies, so the Toraja began placing their dead in tombs high in the cliffs.

Early *tau tau* were stylized figures with almond-shaped eyes and few individualized characteristics. Today, influenced by sculpture from Bali and other islands, the Toraja carve their mortuary effigies to reveal the likeness of the individuals they represent. *Tau tau,* which literally means "little person," is actually a life-size sculpture and is made of several movable pieces so it can be manipulated like a puppet. The best *tau tau* are carved from jackfruit wood, which is treated with coconut oil to give it the tone of the Toraja people's skin. Realism is also evident in the detailed carving of the sexual organs, with the penis always being erect. The figures, though, are dressed before being taken to their resting place and are repaired and reclothed every twenty-five years.

ROCK GRAVES, RANTEPAO

While the Toraja are most famous for the tombs called *keborang batu,* which are cut into limestone cliffs, they bury their dead in other places as well. With the end of tribal warfare in the region, the need for putting graves in hard-to-reach places has lessened (although the growing appreciation of *tau tau* as works of art has recently created a thriving market in stolen Toraja effigies).

Since many people can't afford the expense of cutting caves into cliff faces and the number of spaces left in the mountainsides has dwindled, tombs are often cut into large rocks instead. Smaller and less elaborate, these rock graves haven't room for either the bodies of the dead or full-size *tau tau.* Instead they are markers, more symbols than tombs.

Another unique form of burial is reserved for children who die before cutting their first tooth. These babies are placed in cavities carved into the trunks of living *antolong* trees, which are then covered with sugar-palm fiber. Traditionally, a dog and a pig are slaughtered at the funeral of a young child. Over time, the tree grows over the cavity, leaving scarred bark as a memorial to the dead child.

Today some Toraja are buried in grave houses, wood structures built on flat terrain. These aren't particularly striking or dramatic, but they are certainly easier for the burial crew and can be built anywhere.

CARVINGS

A decorative frieze runs along the top of all four walls of a Toraja rice barn, turning a village feast into a feast for the eyes. Carved and painted wood panels bring the ceremonial event to life: the men wrestling, the water buffalo locking horns in battle, the dog barking, the buffalo being slaughtered, and the villagers marching in procession.

WATER

Once thought to be a series of islands, Sulawesi is a place where the ocean is never far away. Even inland, large lakes such as Poso and Limboto connect people to the water. Aqua-sports, aqua-transit, aqua-culture, aqua-living are everywhere. As a result, everything seems to float: swimmers, boats, little wooden pavilions at the end of narrow piers, small rock islands, even the light of the setting sun.

Bali

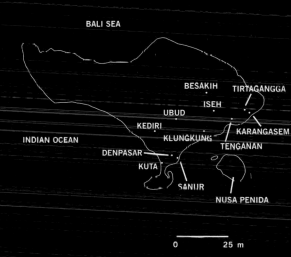

BALI SEA

BESAKIH TIRTAGANGGA

ISEH

UBUD

KEDIRI KARANGASEM

KLUNGKUNG

INDIAN OCEAN TENGANAN

DENPASAR

KUTA

SANUR

NUSA PENIDA

0 — 25 m

Bali is a magnificent repository—of demons, spirits, *leyaks* (witches), multi-armed gods and goddesses, multitiered *meru* (shrine) towers, and outrageously carved temples; of a complex Hindu-Buddhist-animist culture dating from the fifteenth century and still very much alive and kicking; of the collected fantasies of Western travelers and artists who have washed up on its shores for the past hundred years; of what landscape architect Made Wijaya calls the last living classical architecture.

In the United States the only place that evokes the same kind of visceral response is New Orleans, which also has a bizarre mix of cultures, and where humidity,

spice, rice, decay, and fecund growth simultaneously lull and excite one's senses. Like New Orleans, Bali is a place where seemingly rational people believe in spirits. Both places attract more than their fair share of odd characters, charlatans, seekers, and escapees. Somehow both are able to absorb outside influences as powerful as Hinduism and Catholicism, television and tourism, and give them their own special twists.

A 2,171-square-mile island whose heart is a range of impressive volcanoes and whose arteries are clear-water rivers and meticulously engineered irrigation canals, Bali is an intensely farmed rice bowl that supports a population of nearly three million. After hundreds of years of terraced-rice cultivation—for which nearly every square inch of suitable land has been carved and raked into swirling green-and-yellow pyramids of water and earth—Bali's terrain is one of the world's great sculptures. Here the earth itself is a wonderful piece of design: planned, engineered, and maintained by generation after generation.

Rice is the essence of Bali. Every meal spins around a mound of *nasi*. Every family compound has a *lumbung* (rice barn). Every temple festival features multicolored offerings of rice. Wet-rice cultivation

(*sawah*) in this tropical clime brings forth two and sometimes three harvests a year, which has supported for hundreds of years a population density much higher than the wheat-based cultures of ancient and medieval Europe. Since the harnessing of water in complex irrigation systems is necessary for *sawah* farming and such systems require continual repair and tending, the Balinese have developed a finely tuned network of social units called *subak* to oversee it all. Every rice farmer is a member of a *subak* (cooperative), which controls the flow of water from its source to the lowest rice field. Traditionally, the farmer with the lowest-lying land is put in charge of the *subak*, since his survival depends on water flowing along its entire course.

The combination of rich volcanic soil, highly productive rice farming, and easy access to fruit, nuts, and fish has provided the Balinese with a lot of spare time. Scraping a living in places like Europe, Scandinavia, and the Americas was traditionally quite hard. But in a tropical paradise like Bali, the necessities of life have usually come easily—except during the occasional volcanic eruption or devastating typhoon. So the Balinese have always spent a remarkable amount of their time and energy on the arts: architecture, painting, carving in soft *paras* (sandstone) and wood, dance, weaving, and music. The standard line is that every Balinese is an artist—participating in village dances, creating elaborate sculptures or paintings for home and temple, weaving intricate *ikat* textiles, dying colorful batiks, or playing in a *gamelan* orchestra. Girls start dancing the *legong* at five years of age (reaching their prime even younger than Olympic gymnasts). Old ladies weave baskets and textiles. Every man is an architect, designing and building his own house and helping with the village temple.

With the advent of global tourism in the last thirty years, the Balinese have cashed in on these skills by offering up a panoply of tacky and exquisite crafts. What had once been a private or religious activity has now become big business. Some observers bemoan the commercialization of these art forms, but supplying tourists with souvenirs has kept these skills alive. For the most part,

quality has suffered. But the upper end of the market has allowed the most talented Balinese to live entirely off their art and has encouraged them to excel.

Ironically, the moist hot climate of Bali, which pushes the process of decay into hyper-speed, has kept local building traditions and skills alive. Because temples, houses, rice barns, and irrigation systems fall apart so quickly, every generation has had to build anew. While it is almost impossible for even skilled architects in Europe to build cathedrals or aqueducts the way their ancestors did five hundred years ago, the typical Balinese has no trouble replicating a *candi bentar* (split gate) for a temple and doing it the same way as his forefathers from the fifteenth century. And two years after the new gate or bell tower or family temple is completed, it looks as aged and historic as Rheims cathedral. That is not to say that today's Balinese just copy what has been done in the past. Design motifs, carving styles, and artistic themes change with the seasons in Bali. But as Made Wijaya explains in his book *Balinese Architecture: Towards an Encyclopedia,* today's Balinese continue to work within an ancient language of design and construction— incorporating new ideas and influences and keeping that language alive. New materials and methods such as concrete-frame construction, manufactured windows, and air conditioning, though, pose a threat to the long-term viability of the world's

last surviving classical architecture. A high-rise shopping mall in Bali is not a shift in expression that can be absorbed in the local design traditions; it is a violent rip in the architectural fabric itself.

The Balinese universe is an ordered one with everything organized into three realms: gods inhabiting the mountains, demons roaming the seas, and humanity stuck in between. Similarly, buildings are viewed in three parts: the roof, the base, and the building itself. Even the human body has its three divisions with the head being holy, the feet profane, and the torso in between. Consequently, it is considered rude to touch another person's head, where his or her sacred spirit resides. These days, though, things have loosened up a bit, and it is no longer shocking to see someone patting a child on the head or people running their fingers through each other's hair.

Orientation is very important to the Balinese, with the most sacred or important direction being toward the mountains (*kaja*) and the least pure being toward the seas (*kelod*). So when a village is being laid out, its "temple of origin" (*pura puseh*) is built in the *kaja* direction, while the temple of the dead and the cemetery are in the *kelod* direction and the *pura bale agung* (temple of the great meeting hall) is in the center of town. These are but three of the eleven points in the Balinese mandala, and each point is associated with a particular

Hindu god, color, and magical symbol. So powerful is this view of the world that Balinese who travel off the island often feel physically disoriented, even ill, until they can locate *kaja* and *kelod*. But very few Balinese ever feel much desire to leave their island, and most have never journeyed even to Lombok or east Java, just short ferry rides away. When asked if he or she would like to visit other places, the typical Balinese typically shrugs, as if to say, "No. Why would I?"

The traditional Balinese house is not a building but a series of pavilions (*bale*) within a walled compound. Like the layout of the village, the compound is organized along key points of the Balinese mandala—with the family temple in the sacred *kaja* position, the pigsty at *kelod*, and various pavilions pinwheeling around an open courtyard (*natah*). Most of the *bale* are open on at least two sides to allow breezes to pass through and have large thatched roofs supported on wooden posts to provide shade and protection from rain. Parents, grandparents, and unmarried girls usually sleep in a structure called the *menten bandung*, which is enclosed by walls of brick or woven split bamboo, since the family's important belongings are stored here as well. Most of the time people sit in an open *bale*—the women chatting or weaving or preparing the small offerings made several times a day to the gods, the men carving wood or pam-

pering their fighting cocks. The only two-story structure is the *lumbung*, which has a unique curving roof and is raised above a sitting platform to keep the stored rice away from rodents.

The Balinese family structure remains strong today with several generations still living together in compounds. Indeed, foreigners who marry Balinese soon discover, sometimes to their dismay, that they are marrying not an individual but a whole family, even an entire village. Privacy is not an important value and certainly doesn't rank anywhere close to familial and village obligations.

While metal roofs are replacing *alang-alang* thatch and satellite dishes are sprouting everywhere, the *kuren* (Balinese home) lives on, adapting to new ways and habits. Foreign residents have taken long-term leases on some *kuren* (they can't own property) and have found places in these traditional compounds for their computers, libraries, and Western furniture. *Lumbung*

have been emptied of their rice and converted into guest cottages or media rooms. Other foreigners have built their own compounds, adopting some of the old Balinese ways while mixing in influences from abroad. The result is a hybrid design vocabulary in which a wooden Garuda and a Hindu god might sit on a glass-topped table, carved doors from Java and Madura might be hung as decorative panels, and a whirlpool bath might be installed in a traditional outdoor *mandi*.

In places like Ubud and Kuta, many older houses have become *losmen* (homestays), where travelers can spend a night in traditional surroundings. While a Balinese family may still occupy part of the *losmen*, changes are usually made to accommodate foreigners—desks, tables, chairs, and flush toilets are installed, and solid partitions are put up. And, of course, the Balinese themselves have adopted many of these new ways of living—often copying the California-style houses they

see on television. In fact, sometimes it is the foreigner who demands the most Balinese of houses, while the native covets the kind of place a Malibu starlet has. It is not unlike the swap in attire that has happened over the years. A century ago, the Dutch authorities tried to get the bare-breasted Balinese women to put on more clothes. Today it is the westerners who run around the beaches topless and the Balinese who shake their heads.

Bali is a cultural hothouse, supplying rich soil not only for the indigenous Hindu-animist society but for exotic transplants such as foreign adventurers and expatriate artists as well. One of the most colorful of these imports was Donald Friend (born Donald Stuart Leslie Moses), a multitalented Australian who painted, wrote, and entertained outrageously. Usually surrounded by an entourage of Balinese boys, a bottle of gin ever near, Friend was a fixture in Sanur for much of the 1960s, 1970s, and 1980s.

In the late 1960s, Friend joined with Wija Wawo-Runtu, the owner of the Tandjung Sari Hotel, to develop a tract of beachfront property in Sanur into a collection of about a dozen upscale houses. Called Batujimbar, the development helped support Friend's lavish lifestyle and provided him with one of the most beautiful houses on the island. A master plan by the renowned Sri Lankan architect Geoffrey Bawa and a prime location down the road from the chic Tandjung

Sari made Batujimbar a hit with international celebrities, such as Mick Jagger, Jerry Hall, and David Bowie, who rented houses there for extended stays in Bali.

Taking one of the best lots for himself, Friend built a two-story wood *bale* near the beach, using the ground floor as a living room and the loft above as his bedroom. Like any good Balinese compound, Friend's complex eventually included a series of buildings surrounded by walls made of *paras* stone. Although its layout doesn't follow the strict rules of Balinese residential architecture, the compound captures the spirit of local design—creating wonderful indoor-outdoor relationships, orienting its various structures to catch views and breezes, and using traditional materials such as *alang-alang* thatching, bamboo, brick, and *paras* stone. From the split gate (*candi bentar*) at the front of the property to the main house near the beach, this is a special place that blends a painter's sense of composition with a storyteller's love of surprises. Along the way

there are pink stone terraces for lounging after a swim, a small temple for the gods, a rough stone kitchen building with carport, a wooden *bale* sitting on a three-tiered base (perfect for cocktail parties), and an outdoor bathing pavilion tucked in a corner.

The masterpiece of the ensemble is a simple building designed by Bawa—rectangular in plan and made of Majapahit red brick—that is set formally in the center of the compound with a moat around it and a long pool in the front. The ground floor is a single space that was originally Friend's studio and is now an art gallery. Instead of an enclosed second story, there is a covered roof terrace accessed by a set of wide brick stairs on each of the two primary facades. The stairs are unprecedented in Balinese residential architecture but are the

kind of dramatic elements that somehow seem perfect. It was up on this terrace, protected by a traditional bamboo and thatch roof, that Friend would entertain in the late afternoon, extracting as payment a story told or a dream recalled by each of his guests. Everyone would watch the daylight disappear as Friend cried out "Gin here!" at regular intervals. Then with a row of boys behind him, Friend would descend the stairs and lead everyone to a favorite bar in town.

Today the house is owned by Adrian Zecha, the founder of Amanresorts, which runs three hotels on Bali: the Amandari, Amankila, and Amanusa. Usually rented out on a weekly basis, the house seems to miss the flamboyant care of its previous resident, though it still exerts a powerful charm.

Since building the Tandjung Sari Hotel in 1962, Wija Wawo-Runtu has been at the center of the social scene in Sanur. Born into a family of Dutch and Sulawesian heritage, Wawo-Runtu was one of the first entrepreneurs to combine traditional Balinese building techniques with an elegant modern sensibility. The result is a timeless blending of old and new, evidenced both in his hotel and in the house he designed for himself at Batujimbar, the residential community he developed with Donald Friend down the road from the Tandjung Sari.

While the traditional has the upper hand at the Tandjung Sari, a more updated aesthetic holds sway at Wawo-Runtu's house. A painted concrete structure with a thatched roof supported on wood columns, the main house sprouts a master-bedroom wing in the back and a kitchen and servants' wing off the driveway in

the front. Modern elements such as a metal pergola running along the front veranda and simple clean lines establish a framework for Wawo-Runtu's collection of pan-Asian artwork and furniture.

Like traditional Balinese houses, Wawo-Runtu's is entered through a carved stone gate set into a stone wall. Guests then walk along a covered gallery lined on one side with old carved doors hanging from a wooden crossbeam like pictures at an exhibition; the other side is open to the front yard.

The gallery leads to a deep veranda fronting the main house, which serves as a series of outdoor spaces spilling out from indoor rooms. The afternoon sun filters into the veranda through a line of wood birdcages hanging from the metal pergola, the sound of chirping and cackling adding an aural element to the tropical composition.

Water plays an important role here, too, with a narrow channel running along the front and back of the house and turning into a water garden on one side. In the backyard a swimming pool extends perpendicular to the house, pointing toward the beach about one hundred yards away. Between the pool and the Indian Ocean is a small family temple made of stone—an element found at almost every house and building on the island.

Parallel to the pool is the master-bedroom wing, connected to the main house only on the second level. While the main house has guest rooms on the second floor, Wawo-Runtu's private wing has a library above his bedroom.

Furnishings throughout the house reflect the owner's eclectic tastes and wide-ranging travels: a traditional Balinese daybed, colonial wood chairs, bamboo sofas, stone Ganesh statues, Hindu figures, a modern work desk, and Persian drawings. There is even a thoroughly 1990s workout room with exercise equipment, which was installed after Wawo-Runtu suffered a heart attack a few years ago.

Michael White came to Bali from Australia in the 1970s and supported himself teaching tennis to the rich. Soon he was engrossed in the local culture, fascinated by the nuances of local dances and the rich diversity of Balinese temple rituals. In 1979 and 1980, he wrote a regular column, "Stranger in Paradise," for the English-language *Sunday Bali Post,* serving as cultural gadfly fluttering between the equally arcane worlds of temple priests and international jet-setters. Eventually, the tall, red-headed White became fluent in both Indonesian and Balinese (a tricky language that is rarely mastered by foreigners) and took the name Made Wijaya.

Today he is one of the top landscape designers in the country, having shaped the grounds of the Bali Hyatt, the Four Seasons Resort, and the Amandari (all on Bali), and various projects such as the Hyatt Regency in Singapore and David Bowie's house on the island of Mustique in the West Indies. He's also the author of *Balinese Architecture: Towards an Encyclopedia,* a large-format *samzidat* book that is one of the most respected sources on local building and design.

Villa Bebek is his home and office in Sanur. It is a rambling compound of four cottages set within an eclectic jungle of bamboo, flowering plants, small lawns, courtyards, stone terraces, and pantropical elements. The garden design exemplifies Wijaya's self-styled "tropical Cotswold" approach that adapts the English romantic garden to an equatorial climate. It is a place where the picturesque meets the palm. Even Wijaya's name for the house has a subversive touch to it; *bebek* means "duck" in Indonesian, but is also slang for "gay," a sly reference to Wijaya's sexual orientation and a playful nod to his disregard for convention.

Surrounded by stone walls, Villa Bebek turns inward, its buildings looking onto a central courtyard anchored by a swimming pool and a Balinese *kul-kul* (bell tower) that serves as a water tower. As Wijaya's design practice has grown, the ground floors of most of the cottages have become studio space for his employees, while the upstairs are bedrooms for guests.

Local materials, including bamboo, hardwoods, and *alang-alang,* are used throughout the compound, but there is no attempt at purity here. Putty-gray concrete

and ceramic tiles are also part of the mix, and design inspirations come from as far away as North Africa and southern California. One bedroom, for example, has rich Moroccan-blue walls, while another features a "bridal suite" four-poster bed complete with gauzy Victorian curtains. The furnishings are equally eclectic, ranging from Chinese chests and shields from Irian Jaya to a campy matador lamp picked up in Los Angeles. Wijaya's use of assertive colors on interior surfaces and garden walls and his inventive combinations of diverse elements are hardly typical of Balinese design. But his skillful weaving of indoors with outdoors makes everything seem to fit in this southeast corner of Bali. Classical Balinese architecture is left for his book; Villa Bebek is where Made Wijaya mixes a bubbly cocktail of design.

RICE FIELDS

Thanks to a tropical climate, the Balinese can pull two and sometimes three rice harvests a year from the land. And unlike many other parts of the world where planting and harvesting happen at the same time for all farmers, in Bali the timing of the growing cycle varies from one *subak* (farming cooperative) to another. So a day's drive along country roads in Bali brings with it views of paddies at all stages of development—from recently plowed mud to the vibrant yellows and greens of rice plants waving in the wind.

DOORS

In the well-ordered Balinese universe, moving from one type of space to another is usually marked with a flourish. Go from a street to a family compound and you must pass through a decorated door. Go from the outer coutyard of a temple to the inner areas and a *candi bentar* (split gate) announces the transition. Always eager to delight the senses, the Balinese see doors as a perfect excuse to carve, paint, and embellish.

Tucked behind the sprawling grounds of the Bali Hyatt, off a narrow *gang* (dirt road), the Carpenter-Vooges compound unfolds as a series of architectural hybrids: a main house that started as a typical Balinese structure and has acquired a kitchen and veranda, a wooden guest cottage built on stilts, a Balinese *paon* (kitchen) transformed into servants' quarters, and, last, a building made of wooden walls salvaged from old Javanese houses. Bali itself is a land of hybrids—Hindu/Buddhist, magical/mundane, traditional/modern—so mixing and matching seems a proper way of doing things here.

An author and art consultant, Bruce Carpenter first came to Indonesia twenty years ago with a backpack, bumming around Asia like so many others at the time. His wife, Carola Vooges, is a designer of clothes, objects, and interiors. Together they designed their family compound using local craftspeople to build the houses, combining elements from various parts of Asia, and furnishing it with an eclectic mix of Chinese, Indonesian, and southeast Asian art.

Attracted to Sanur's history of European artists in residence and its place in local lore as a haunting ground for *leyaks* (witches), Carpenter and Vooges leased the property in the fall of 1992 and started working on the brick main house. After adding a new kitchen and veranda, they ripped out the shiny white

floor tiles inside the house and put in old turquoise-, celadon-, and peach-colored cement tiles like the ones they found in pre-1960s local houses. "Our Balinese landlord was shocked," recalls Carpenter, "because all the new houses had hospital-white tiles."

Next they remodeled the old Balinese kitchen building into bedrooms for the servants, covering the brick with mud and thatching the roof with elephant grass. Although structures made entirely of mud were once common in Bali, building them today is a dying art, says Carpenter.

Needing space for friends who dropped by, Carpenter and Vooges built a Malay-style wooden house raised on stilts so air can circulate around it and keep it cool. Balinese houses, on the other hand, are usually built on stone or brick platforms but are often open on two or three sides to keep them cool.

In the 1980s, as the Indonesian economy took off and a growing middle class acquired the trappings of a more modern and Western lifestyle, traditional houses went out of fashion in many parts of Java. Old residences started disappearing at a rapid clip. Although many of the houses were brick, they all had a wooden wall known as a *gebyog* that divided the living room in the front from the main bedroom in the rear. Consisting of three panels—usually made of teak—these *gebyog* were often elaborately carved affairs with a door in the

center and solid panels on either side. "I wanted a wood house and I love teak," says Carpenter. "But I didn't want to chop down the rain forest to get it."

So he started buying *gebyog* as old houses in Java were being torn down, eventually acquiring about a dozen. He shipped them to Bali, then stored them for nearly two years until he could expand the size of his compound with the addition of an adjacent parcel of land.

Once the property was acquired, Carpenter and Vooges learned that building a house from old wood panels, most of which were warped or uneven, was no easy feat. Fortunately, the Balinese are skilled wood-workers and could craft special pieces of wood to make everything fit. The next problem was getting a uniform

finish for the panels, each of which had a different patina. After much experimenting, Carpenter devised a fifteen-step process that included a lot of washing and scrubbing, then sanding, more washing, and rubbing with dry limewash, melamine, dirt, and sand. Burnt sienna, gold leaf, and cinnabar were applied for color, then everything was treated with a mild acid solution and rubbed with wax and oil.

Not wanting to re-create the small dark rooms of most Javanese houses, Carpenter laid out his new wood house with three comfortably sized rooms and a deep veranda on the front. It is a simple but striking design that now serves as the compound's master-bed-room wing, freeing up the main house for the couple's two children.

TANDJUNG SARI HOTEL, SANUR

One of the first great luxury hotels in Bali, the Tandjung Sari is most impressive for its sense of restraint. With twenty-nine individual bungalows, each with its own garden, the place is intimate in size and demeanor. There is a swimming pool, a dining pavilion, and a thatched-roof bar facing the beach, but otherwise it seems more like a rich friend's island retreat than a hotel.

Started in 1962 by Wija Wawo-Runtu, the Tandjung Sari was built by Balinese craftspeople using local materials: bamboo, *alang-alang* thatching, carved wood doors, and *paras* stone for outdoor terraces and garden walls. While many of the upscale hotels that came after it laid on Balinese decor with a heavy hand, the Tandjung Sari captures the essence of the local design tradition without lavishly following all of the rules. The individual bungalows are carefully oriented to views and revolve around the hotel's central pool, dining, and bar area, but there is no attempt to mimic the plan of a traditional Balinese compound. Likewise, stone walls and small gardens define and enclose outdoor spaces, but there is no pretense that this is a large family residence. Local textiles and crafts are used with discretion, not garishly displayed to create a themed-entertainment experience.

The spirit of the Tandjung Sari is perhaps best grasped at the reception pavilion—a perfectly crafted Balinese *bale* enveloped by gardens and stone walls. A small wooden desk, like one from a prosperous trader's office, is where guests sign in—a far cry from the grandiose lobbies of most expensive hotels. From this small outdoor pavilion there is no view of the hotel itself or even the beach beyond, just a stone path leading through a lush garden. The result is a wonderful sense of anticipation tinged with mystery, a feeling that one has arrived at someplace special.

THE CHEDI, UBUD

Although Bali is an island with some beautiful beaches, its heart and soul lie in the mountainous region near its geographic center. Drawn to the cooler climes of the hills and the life-giving spirits that dwell in the mountains, the Balinese have terraced the sloping terrain here with rice paddies and filled the valleys with thriving villages. The town of Ubud has long been a hub of artistic activity, a status that the European artists who came in the 1920s only reinforced.

Just a few miles outside of Ubud, the Chedi clings to the hillsides overlooking the Ayung River, perched above a valley thick with trees and wildlife. Designed by the Australian architecture firm Kerry Hill Associates, the Chedi is a hotel nestled into its natural setting. Beautiful gray river stones are the dominant building material, giving the Chedi a solidity unusual in a place where most residential buildings are open and ethereal. But the Chedi's thick stone walls and narrow pathways evoke the feeling of walking through a Balinese village where stone and brick walls surround individual family compounds.

Opened in April 1996, the Chedi has just fifty-four rooms in two-story buildings and six individual suites. The two-story buildings are tucked into the hillsides, so rooms on both floors are entered from what appears to be the ground level. This allows all rooms to open onto outdoor spaces.

Fitting into the landscape is what this hotel is all about. The main public structures—including the lobby pavilion, restaurant, and swimming pool—are all terraced into the site, providing spectacular views of the Ayung River valley. Likewise, the residential buildings curve along a bend in the river, so every guest room gets a view to the valley. Modern in its design and traditional in its respect for the land, the Chedi allows guests to appreciate the remarkable place in which it is set.

100%

BARONG DANCE

Although bug-eyed and fearsome looking, the Barong is a benevolent beast who can clown around one moment then turn serious once danger arrives. In this traditional Balinese dance, evil is personified by Rangda, an ugly old witch who has the bad habit of kidnapping lovely princesses and putting good-guy warriors into trances so they turn their daggers upon themselves. But the Barong always chases Rangda away, saving the day.

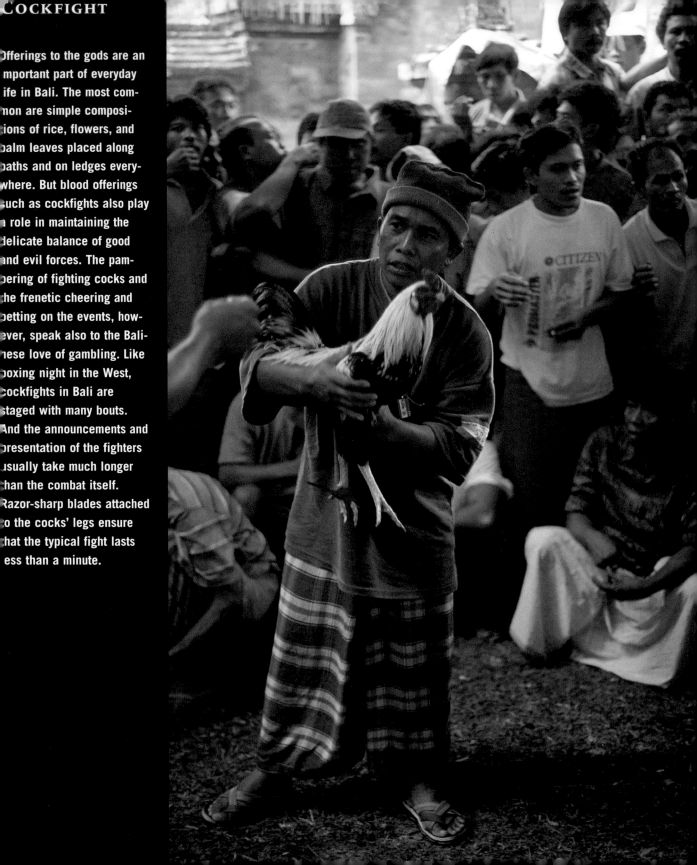

COCKFIGHT

Offerings to the gods are an important part of everyday life in Bali. The most common are simple compositions of rice, flowers, and palm leaves placed along paths and on ledges everywhere. But blood offerings such as cockfights also play a role in maintaining the delicate balance of good and evil forces. The pampering of fighting cocks and the frenetic cheering and betting on the events, however, speak also to the Balinese love of gambling. Like boxing night in the West, cockfights in Bali are staged with many bouts. And the announcements and presentation of the fighters usually take much longer than the combat itself. Razor-sharp blades attached to the cocks' legs ensure that the typical fight lasts less than a minute.

Throw a coconut in any direction at this multifamily compound in Sanur and you are bound to hit a writer or publisher. Begun by journalist Leonard Lueras in the late 1980s, before prices in the area skyrocketed, the place is a favorite resting stop for the foreign press. On any given day the four houses and accompanying rice barns might be occupied by a Magnum photographer, someone from the Asian edition of *Time* magazine, Didiet Millet (the Singapore-based publisher of Editions Didiet Millet), Tom Chapman (who has his own publishing house in Hong Kong), ceramic designer Brent Hesselyn, lawyer Tom Morgan, and Lueras. "For a while we had three writers here," relates Lueras. "We called it 'the Writers' Block,' because none of us were writing."

The official name is Taman Mertasari: *taman* means "garden" and *mertasari,* which is the old name for this part of Sanur, means "essence of holy water." Lueras, who was born in New Mexico and raised in California, first came to Bali for rest and relaxation during his days as a correspondent covering the Vietnam war for the *Honolulu Advertiser.* "We'd come here and surf," he recalls. Lueras hasn't covered a war in years, but he still surfs and recently wrote a guide to surfing in Indonesia with his son Lorca. And despite all the natural and human-made distractions on the island, he's managed to write, photograph, edit, or produce some twenty books on Asia, including *Bali: The Ultimate Island.*

"When we started building here, it was just cows and pigs and trees," remembers Lueras. Pooling resources with Hesselyn and then two other friends, he put up a wall around the property and dug a well. Each person built his own house and together they added a swimming pool and a few ancillary pavilions. Three types of rice barns—two *lumbungs,* a *jinan,* and a *glebug*—were transported in pieces from various parts of Bali and then reassembled in what Lueras jokingly refers to as his "upmarket hippie commune." The barns don't store rice anymore, but instead serve as bedroom, library, and television/media room.

The main houses reflect the interests and idiosyncrasies of their occupants. Hesselyn's is painted a mango orange and has dozens of Balinese bells hung from the eaves. Lueras's is really two pavilions united by one long thatched roof and a lovely sitting room in the

middle that is open on two sides. Two bedrooms and a kitchen are on the ground floor, while upstairs is Lueras's domain: a Soho loft cum Balinese pavilion that works as bedroom, living room, and office.

Neither Lueras nor any of the other people involved in Taman Mertasari is an architect, so they all relied on the time-tested method of "construction by demolition," says Lueras sardonically. "You put something up and if you don't like it, you pull it down and do it again."

Few buildings in Bali have as rich a history as this tiny house with the giant view. Built as a studio by the German painter/musicologist/arts promoter Walter Spies, who lived in Bali from 1927 to 1942, it subsequently was occupied by the painter Theo Meyer, a wife of Raja Gede Dangin, and the Italian socialite Idana Pucci. In 1995 Hugo Jereissati, a Brazilian who has spent much of the last twenty years in Bali, took the place over and fixed it up.

Over the years, what had begun as a one-room rural studio has grown into a charming cluster of small buildings: a two-bedroom guest house, a kitchen pavilion, and a freestanding wing with master bedroom and maid's quarters. The original studio is now the dining room; it is attached to the guest house by a common terrace and roof.

The village of Iseh is still remote, connected to the main thoroughfare between Ubud and Candi Dasa by a rugged, winding mountain road. "Thank God the road is so bad," says Jereissati. "It keeps the tourists away." A small square with an unassuming temple marks the center of the village, which has changed little in decades. A simple concrete gate with a red door and checkered Balinese banners is all that announces the Spies house from the street.

Once past the gate, you walk along a path that leads between the guest house and the master-bedroom wing. The buildings and landscaping are tightly arranged, creating a sense of intimacy with nature and architecture. There is no front door to any of the buildings, just covered walkways onto which rooms open. What pulls you forward, past the guest rooms and dining room, is the light at the end—a hint of Balinese scenery. When you get to the terrace, it hits you—the same spectacular view that brought Spies to this remote spot: terraced rice paddies, patches of corn and chili fields, growths of salek

and coconut trees, and the looming presence of Gunung Agung, the holy volcano of Bali. One of Spies's most famous paintings, *Morning in Iseh*, depicts this view, and it is as accurate today as it was in the 1930s.

Rather than build in the traditional Balinese way, Spies and the people who have added onto his studio have used a design vocabulary that seems universal in its simplicity: plain concrete forms faced with plaster, clay-tile roofs, wide overhanging eaves, and slender wooden columns. The walls are painted a dark, muted pink, which is common in this area but nowhere else in Bali, says Jereissati. "It reminds me of houses in Brazil." Doors and shutters are carved and painted wood, providing visual accents to the otherwise plain surfaces.

Before he moved in, Jereissati rebuilt the roofs of the house and renovated the wing where he sleeps, turning four small spaces into a large master bedroom and a room for the staff. A local architect, Made Nasib, worked with him to fix up the place. Interiors throughout the house were also redone, using an eclectic but harmonious mix of canopy beds, tropical furniture, ceramic tile floors, and great wooden chests.

Now Jereissati is working on the landscaping around the house, adding flowering plants such as hibiscus and frangipani along a steep path to the rice fields. "Everything is so green here, you need to add some color." He is also starting to grow plants he can use in cooking, "all sorts of leafy and spicy things."

"My European friends are always interested in the jungle, the greenery here," says Jereissati. "As a Brazilian, I almost take the greenery for granted. I'm less interested in the jungle, the primitive aspects of Indonesia, and more interested in the culture, which is incredibly vibrant and alive."

Like Spies before him, Jereissati uses the house as a retreat from the more hectic parts of Bali, but also as a magical place to entertain. It is hard to say no to an invitation to enjoy drinks, dinner, and company at a place with such a view—no matter how tortuous the drive might be.

A royal folly built in the tradition of Chinese water palaces (and their European imitators such as Kew Gardens in England), Tirtagangga is a fanciful complex of pavilions and pools fed by a sacred spring. Although it has the air of something built in a previous century and now pleasantly decaying, Tirtagangga was erected in 1948 by the last raja of Karangasem, Anak Agung Agung Anglurah Ketut Karangasem, who seems to have been quite a water enthusiast, having built another water palace in Ujung in the 1920s.

On a terraced hillside overlooking Tirtagangga, the Australian designer Carole Muller has built herself a small house—simple in plan and open to views of the royal playground below. Resting on the foundations of a previous structure, the house has just two main rooms—each furnished with a large four-poster bed and opening onto a veranda paved with cream-colored ceramic tiles set within stone borders. Painted-canvas sliding screens can separate the two rooms, but most of

the time they are open so the house feels like one large space. And when the glass-and-wood wall panels that wrap around two sides of the house are open, the interiors practically melt away, becoming merely covered extensions of the outdoors.

Slipped behind the main rooms of the house are bathrooms with outdoor bathing areas and a tiny alcove used by Muller as a home office. Beyond these facilities is a two-story tower for the servants and an attached kitchen.

Sharing the view of the water palace with the main house is a small dining pavilion raised two steps above the common terrace. Open all around and surrounded on three sides by a lotus pool, the dining pavilion echoes the architecture of the follies it overlooks. Lunch in the pavilion or on the terrace, with the sounds of Balinese children frolicking in the pools below, is one of the more carefree experiences one can enjoy in this world.

TRADITIONAL FAMILY COMPOUND, KEDIRI

The family home of I Gusti Oka, southwest of Ubud, is a classic example of traditional Balinese architecture adapted to the real world with a few twentieth-century anachronisms. All the rules of Balinese residential design were followed in laying out this compound—from the placement of the family temple (*sanggah*) in the *kaja* (mountainside) location and the kitchen (*paon*) closest to *kelod* (seaward) to the arrangement of the various *bale* around a ceremonial pavilion (*bale dangin*). Enclosed by a brick wall, the compound is entered through a stone gate where colorful offerings of rice, flowers, and banana leaves are left several times a day to welcome good spirits. Just inside the gate is a freestanding *aling-aling* wall, forcing guests to turn either left or right and, more important, preventing evil spirits from entering. (Spooks, of course, can only move in straight lines.) Although traditional in design, this home is not a museum. In several of the old-fashioned *bale* are television sets sitting next to old carvings, bell-shaped baskets for holding fighting cocks, or maybe a wooden birdcage. And a new driveway next to the formal entry houses the family car.

I Gusti Oka is a banker who has also done well in real estate and now spends most of his time in Denpasar. But his uncle Gusti Made Rai and many of his older relatives still live here at the family compound, where important rites such as births, tooth filings (done at adolescence to remove the animal-like points of one's canine teeth), marriages, and deaths are honored. The old people here live much as they have for centuries—preparing temple offerings on the wood platforms under the rice barn, relaxing in a shaded bale during the hottest parts of the day, pampering the fighting roosters, and preparing meals in the wood-fired stove. Watching Indonesian soap operas on television and calling the children on the phone may be new, but the essential rhythms of life haven't changed much.

BASKET WEAVER'S STUDIO, TENGANAN

Bali Aga is the term used to refer to the original civilization of Bali that predated the spread of Hinduism and Majapahit culture from Java in the thirteenth century. Animist and rooted in the worship of spirits found in mountains, water, trees, and such, this ancient culture retreated to a few isolated villages after the Majapahit court moved east to Bali, in the wake of Islam's triumph in Java in the fifteenth century. What survives of Bali's original civilization are the archaic Bali Aga villages, such as Tenganan in the eastern part of the island.

Land in Tenganan is owned in common by the village, and the rich rice fields today are worked by hired labor, freeing residents to concentrate on their remarkable handicrafts: *lontar* books made of dried palm leaves, carvings, and, most famously, *geringsing,* the double *ikat* textile in which the fabric's pattern is dyed into both the warp and weft fibers before it is meticulously woven.

Tenganan also has some fine basket makers, one of whom is Wayan Kadep, who specializes in using a particular type of vine with black markings. In a feat similar to that of *geringsing* weavers, Kadep weaves these vines into baskets so that their natural markings create patterns—arrows, zigzags, lines, and diamonds.

Kadep's compound is set within beautiful stone walls off the village's wide dirt boulevard. In front is the gallery with several open pavilions where baskets are displayed on wooden platforms that are raised a couple of steps off the ground. In the back is his studio, where as many as twenty-five people work. This is time-consuming labor. A small-to medium-sized basket can take two weeks to make, a large one as much as four months. The compound has a rugged beauty made pure by its reliance on the most basic elements: stone, wood, and earth.

TAMAN GILI, KLUNGKUNG

Bali was the last major Indonesian island to fall to the Dutch, and the kingdom of Klungkung in the eastern part of the island was the last major Balinese power to confront the Dutch army. In April 1908, the raja of Klungkung, his entire family, and court—all dressed in white, the color of death—marched out of the royal palace and faced the European invaders. After the raja was shot and killed, the other Balinese took out their sacred *krises* (knives) and killed themselves, as the Dutch razed the great palace of Klungkung, the most powerful state on the island.

What's left of the palace is the Taman Gili. Now a tranquil oasis within a bustling city, the Taman Gili features two superb examples of Balinese palace architecture—the Bale Kambang (floating pavilion) surrounded by a lily-filled moat and the Bale Kerta Gosa (hall of justice). Under the raja, the Bale Kambang was the headquarters of the royal guard and the Bale Kerta Gosa was where the raja would consult with his advisers. After the Dutch took over, judges in criminal cases would meet in the Bale Kerta Gosa, as defendants waited anxiously in the Bale Kambang.

Both of the buildings are renowned for the intricate paintings executed on the inside surfaces of their ceilings and done in the Kamasan style, reminiscent of scenes in *wayang kulit* puppet shows. The stories recorded in the paintings unfold in horizontal bands wrapping around all four sides of the ceilings and stacked one on top of the other until they reach the ridge beam of the roof. The more famous paintings are in the Bale Kerta Gosa and depict the adventures of Bima, one of the Pandawa brothers from the *Mahabharata,* as he travels from hell to heaven in search of a magical potion that will impart immortality to his parents. Both the Bale Kambang and the Bale Kerta Gosa have been extensively rebuilt and their paintings redone several times this century.

TEMPLES

The number of temples (*pura*) in Bali never fails to astonish foreigners. Every family compound has a temple. Most villages have at least three. And scattered throughout the island are special temples dedicated to particular gods or spirits as well as temples such as Pura Besakih (the mother temple), which are part of the patrimony of all Balinese. The settings for some *pura* are magical: on the slopes of volcanoes, surrounded by moats, or cut off from the island completely at high tide.

Loud, joyous affairs, cremations in Bali celebrate a soul's release from its earthly body and its return to heaven. Preparations for these spectacles often take months, during which time the body of the deceased is temporarily buried. On the day of the cremation, the body is blessed at the temple of the dead, then placed onto a funeral tower made of bamboo, paper, and bright fabric. The tower, strapped to a bamboo grid, is hoisted on the shoulders of a crew of black-clad men, shaken wildly to disorient the soul of the dead person, then paraded to the cremation grounds. A bamboo and paper sarcophagus in the shape of an animal (usually a bull) is given the same treatment, as well as a rowdy dousing of water from large hoses. Since cremations are expensive events, it is common for poorer families to pool their resources or to wait until a wealthy person dies and then participate in that grand affair. At the cremation grounds the tower, sarcophogus, and body are set ablaze. Later the ashes are taken to the sea and poured into the water.

Marry a Balinese princess and you get a house at the royal palace, just behind a Chinese-inspired water pavilion and a European-style official residence. That's what Carl Burman, a nice Jewish boy from California, did a few years ago. Now the couple and their child live part of the year at Karangasem Palace in east Bali, where Mirah's grandfather, Anak Agung Agung Anglurah Ketut Karangasem, the last raja of Karangasem, resided until his death in 1966.

A red-brick tower marks the entrance to the palace and leads to a small dirt courtyard and another tower. Through the tower gate and to the right is the main courtyard of the palace. On one side of the shaded yard is the Bale London, a late-nineteenth-century building loosely modeled after English baroque architecture that housed the raja's bedroom and office. Uninhabited since the raja died, the Bale London is a faded yellow rose of a building, evocative of a more luxurious time of royal prerogative. On the other side of the courtyard are the Bale Pemandesan (a small wooden pavilion used for ceremonies), the Bale Pewedaan (reserved for a Balinese holy man),

and the Bale Kambang or ("house on the water")
sitting in the center of a large pool and reached by
an arching stone bridge.

Behind these official structures are the less formal,
more ad hoc houses where relatives of the late raja
live—including the Burmans and Mirah's brother Anak
Anak Made Arya, who works for the Indonesian Depart-
ment of Culture and Education. The Burmans' house is
called Gedong Yogya, after a large wooden
birdcage that was given many years ago by the raja of

Yogyakarta in exchange for a Balinese *gamelan* orchestra.

Built, rebuilt, and remodeled many times over the
years, the Burmans' house is a hodgepodge of styles,
decorative touches, and spaces that somehow coalesces
with a quirky charm. The Burmans have added such
eccentric elements as an egg-shaped dome on top of an
old pitched roof, a freestanding arcade clad with pieces
of mirror, and mosaic-encrusted doorways. The overall
effect is a combination of 1960s funk-a-delic and tropical vernacular, a kind of Berkeley-meets-Bali design.

"The garden is more important than the house," states Jean-François Fichot of his residence on the wooded outskirts of Ubud. "In a place like Bali you spend most of your time outdoors." In the seven years he has lived here, Fichot has spent a great deal of time outdoors, creating not one but a series of gardens that flow seamlessly one into the other. The result is an intricate procession of outdoor experiences that at first glance seems purely natural, as if Fichot merely cleared away a few areas for a house, a pool, and a guest cottage, and left everything else as he had found it. Hardly. All this beautiful scenery took lots of hard work.

While many of the plants are indigenous to this area—bamboo, coconut palms, and various fruit trees—Fichot brought quite a few from around the tropics. There are the manoi plants from Tahiti with their star-shaped flowers, bromeliads from Latin America, avocados from the New World, and cannonball trees from South America. There are also ginger, passionflower, jasmine, and night queen—all working together to create a private jungle that is delightfully wild despite all its careful cultivation.

To gain access to this lush realm, guests walk over a modern bridge, designed by noted Balinese architect Amir Rabik, crossing a thickly wooded ravine. From the start, it is clear you are entering a special place, a world apart from the increasingly congested streets of Ubud. A narrow stone path leads up a hill, around the swimming pool, and to the main house.

A jewelry designer, Fichot has a gallery on the ground floor of the main house, with his bedroom above. Off the bedroom is a small roof terrace where he can enjoy spectacular views of his neighbors' rice fields stretching into the distance. In front of the house is a large lotus pond populated by a swarm of colorful koi and bordered on two sides by a wooden walkway that connects with the guest house. A Balinese architect, Kadec Arto, helped Fichot with the design of the houses.

Fichot had traveled a lot in India in the 1970s, then visited New York City in 1978, where he saw a Balinese dance performance at Carnegie Hall. "I fell in love with Bali that night," he remembers. "I said, 'I have to go there.'" It's been his home ever since.

GLOSSARY

adat custom, tradition

alang-alang a common variety of grass widely used for roof thatching

Aluk Todolo traditional religion of the Toraja people in Sulawesi

alun-alun public square of a town, particularly the square in front of a *kraton* in Java

Asmat indigenous group in Irian Jaya

bale Balinese pavilion, house, or meeting hall

bale dangin ceremonial pavilion in the center of a Balinese family compound

Bali Aga original Balinese, whose civilization predates the Majapahit immigration from Java in the fourteenth and fifteenth centuries; villages such as Tenganan in east Bali remain active centers of Bali Aga culture

banjar district of a Balinese village in which social and community activities are based

banyan holy tree, also called *waringin*, often found at temples and important places such as an *alun-alun*

Barong mythical beast with features of a lion and a dog; the hero of the Balinese Barong dance

batik traditional cloth made using a resist-dye technique

becak trishaw; common form of transportation throughout the archipelago

bilik sleeping room in a Minangkabau house

Brahma one of the three most important Hindu gods; the creator

Bugis seafaring people from Sulawesi; originally infamous as pirates

candi Hindu temple or shrine in Java and Bali

candi bentar split gate at entry to a Balinese temple

dalang puppet master in a *wayang kulit* shadow puppet show

dalem the back of a Javanese house

gamelan traditional orchestra of mostly percussion instruments, such as xylophones and gongs; found in Java and Bali

Ganesha elephant-headed Hindu god; son of Shiva

gang alley or dirt path

Garuda mythical creature with a bird's body and a man's head; Vishnu's mount; national symbol of Indonesia

gebyog carved wood wall in traditional Javanese house, dividing the living room in the front from the bedroom in the back

geringsing double *ikat* cloth, made by dying both warp and weft strands before being woven; made in only a few Bali Aga villages, such as Tenganan

ijuk black fiber from the sugar palm used for thatching

ikat cloth in which strands are dyed before being woven into a pattern

istana palace

joglo traditional four-columned Javanese roof

kaja toward the mountains; the holiest direction in Bali

kampung neighborhood or village compound

keborang batu cliff tombs of the Tonga people in Sulawesi

kelod toward the sea; least pure direction in Bali

kraton Javanese palace, usually encompassing an entire city district

kris traditional curved-bladed dagger, often passed down as an heirloom from one generation to another; usually believed to have spiritual power

kul-kul Balinese bell tower

kuren Balinese house

legong classical Balinese dance performed by two young girls and a servant

leyak a witch in Bali

lontar a type of palm; also the books written on palm leaves

losmen a Balinese homestay or family compound with rooms rented to travelers

lumbung rice barn

Mahabharata Hindu epic recounting the fight between the Pandavas and the Kauravas; many *wayang kulit* puppet shows and much Hindu art depict scenes from this great tale

Majapahit Hindu dynasty originally based in Java, then pushed to Bali in the fourteenth century after its defeat by Islamic forces

mandi Balinese bath, usually outdoors

menten bandung building in a Balinese family compound where parents, grandparents, and unmarried girls sleep

meru multiroofed shrines, thatched with *ijuk*, found at Balinese temples; the number of roofs is always odd, with the highest being eleven

nasi rice

natah courtyard of a Balinese family compound

niskala in Bali, the occult world

paon Balinese kitchen

paras soft sandstone used for buildings and sculpture

pasar market

pendopo large, many-columned pavilion in Java, used for receiving guests

pinisi Bugis schooner

prahu traditional outrigger boat

pura bale agung temple in the center of a Balinese compound

pura puseh Balinese temple

puri palace

Ramadan holy month in the Muslim calendar, when people fast during the day and eat only in the evening

Ramayana Hindu epic story of Prince Rama and his adventures in defeating the evil king Ravana

rangda Balinese witch

rendang spicy Sumatran beef dish, a staple at Padang restaurants

rijsttafel Dutch-Indonesian banquet with many different dishes served at the same time

rumah adat traditional house

rumah gadang traditional family house of the Minangkabau people in Sumatra

rumah lima traditional river house in Palembang, Sumatra

sanggah family temple in a Balinese residential compound

sawah wet-rice cultivation

sekala in Bali, the material world

sentong ceremonial area in a Balinese family compound

Shiva Hindu god; the destroyer, but also honored as the one who clears the way for rebirth

songket handwoven cloth with silver or gold thread

soto ayam chicken soup

subak cooperative organization that maintains rice fields in Bali

surau in the Minangkabau area of Sumatra, a house where boys and unmarried men live

taman garden

tau tau carved funeral effigies placed outside the cliff graves of the Toraja people in Sulawesi

tolak angin carved and fretted wood gables that slope outward from houses in North Sumatra; literally "shield against the wind"

tongkonan Toraja family house or house of origin

Vishnu Hindu god; the preserver

Wallace Line named after the nineteenth-century naturalist Alfred Russel Wallace, this line runs between Bali and Lombok and then Borneo and Sulawesi and marks the division of Asia from Australasia in terms of flora and fauna

wantilan communal pavilion in a Balinese village

warung food stall or inexpensive restaurant/convenience store

wayang kulit shadow-puppet show